Basic accounting 1

Workbook

David Cox

Michael Fardon

osborne
BOOKS

Published by Osborne Books Limited
Unit 1B Everoak Estate
Bromyard Road
Worcester WR2 5HP
Tel 01905 748071
Email books@osbornebooks.co.uk
Website www.osbornebooks.co.uk

Design by Laura Ingham
Cover and page design image © Istockphoto.com/Petrovich9

Printed by CPI Antony Rowe Limited, Chippenham

British Library Cataloguing in Publication Data
A catalogue record for this book is available from the British Library

ISBN 978 1905777 433

Contents

Chapter activities

Chapter activities – answers

Practice assessments

Practice assessments – answers

Acknowledgements

The publisher wishes to thank the following for their help with the reading and production of the book: Jean Cox, Jon Moore and Cathy Turner. Thanks are also due to Roger Petheram for his technical editorial work and to Laura Ingham for her designs for this series.

The publisher is indebted to the Association of Accounting Technicians for its kind permission for the reproduction of its sample assessment in this text.

Authors

David Cox has more than twenty years' experience teaching accountancy students over a wide range of levels. Formerly with the Management and Professional Studies Department at Worcester College of Technology, he now lectures on a freelance basis and carries out educational consultancy work in accountancy studies. He is author and joint author of a number of textbooks in the areas of accounting, finance and banking.

Michael Fardon has extensive teaching experience of a wide range of banking, business and accountancy courses at Worcester College of Technology. He now specialises in writing business and financial texts and is General Editor at Osborne Books. He is also an educational consultant and has worked extensively in the areas of vocational business curriculum development.

Introduction

what this book covers

This book has been written specifically to provide practice assessment material for the AAT Learning Area 'Basic Accounting I' which combines three QCF Units:

- Principles of recording and processing financial transactions
- Preparing and recording financial documentation
- Processing ledger transactions and extracting a trial balance

what this book contains

This book is set out in two sections:

- **Chapter activities** which provide extra practice material in addition to the activities included in the Osborne Books Tutorial text. Answers to the Chapter activities are set out in this book.
- **Practice assessments** are included to prepare the student for the Computer Based Assessments. They are based directly on the structure, style and content of the sample assessment material provided by the AAT at www.aat.org.uk. Suggested answers to the Practice Assessments are set out in this book.

online support from Osborne Books

This book is supported by practice material available at www.osbornebooks.co.uk

This material is available to tutors – and to students at their discretion – in two forms:

- A **Tutor Zone** which is available to tutors who have adopted the Osborne Books texts. This area of the website provides extra assessment practice material (plus answers) in addition to the activities included in this Workbook text.
- **Online learning** – online practice questions designed to familiarise students with the style of the AAT Computer Based Assessments

further information

If you want to know more about our products, please visit www.osbornebooks.co.uk, email books@osbornebooks.co.uk or telephone Osborne Books Customer Services on 01905 748071.

Chapter activities

1

Chapter activities
Introduction to the accounting system

1.1 A sale for immediate settlement made at a shop using a bank debit card is known as a

	✔
cash sale	
credit sale	
debit sale	

Tick the appropriate box.

1.2 An entry in a book of prime entry is:

	✔
an entry in the ledger accounts of a business	
an entry in the trial balance of a business	
the first place an entry is recorded in the accounting records	

Tick the appropriate box.

1.3 The 'ledger' system of accounts is normally set up for recording:

	✔
cash transactions only	
cash and credit transactions only	
cash and credit and other financial transactions	

Tick the appropriate box.

1.4   A sales ledger control account contains the totals of accounts of:

	✔
customers who buy goods and services on a cash basis	
customers who buy goods and services on a credit basis	
suppliers who provide goods and services on a cash basis	
suppliers who provide goods and services on a credit basis	

Tick the appropriate box.

1.5   Select the missing words from the selection below to complete the following text:

A .... sets out in two columns the balances of the

.. of a business.

The .... of the two columns should .... The debit column

includes the accounts of .... and the credit column includes the accounts of

.. This provides the .... of a business with important and

useful financial information.

Choose from:

payables	**agree**	**ledger accounts**	**managers**
receivables	**totals**	**trial balance**	

2	Chapter activities Financial documents for sales

2.1 Praxis Stationery has supplied the following goods to a credit customer, Dover Designs.

The list price of the goods is £4.00 per box file, plus VAT at 17.5%. Dover Designs is to be given a 20% trade discount and a 2% discount for settlement within 14 days.

DELIVERY NOTE   **No** 246

PRAXIS STATIONERY   **Date** 09 07 20-3
45 Jarvis Street
Mereford MR1 2GH

Dover Designs
68 Whitecliff Street, Granstow, GR3 7GH   Customer code DO109

---

100 Box files, Code BX100

(a)   You are to complete the following invoice

INVOICE   **No** 1689

PRAXIS STATIONERY   **Date** 09 07 20-3
45 Jarvis Street
Mereford MR1 2GH
VAT Reg 831 8627 06

To
Dover Designs
68 Whitecliff Street, Granstow, GR3 7GH   Customer code

                                                   Delivery note no

Quantity	Product code	Unit price (£)	Total (£)	Net (£)	VAT (£)	Total (£)

(b)   If Dover Designs does not settle the invoice within 14 days, Dover designs will have to pay Praxis Stationery a total of:

✔

£374.88	
£368.48	
£376.00	

Tick the appropriate box.

2.2   The following transactions have been passed through the account of a Rosetti Associates, a new credit customer of Praxis Limited:

Date	Document	Amount (£)
1 August	Invoice 1748	4,567.89
9 August	Invoice 1778	2,457.60
10 August	Invoice 1783	4,678.30
17 August	Credit note 319	280.50
29 August	Cheque	4,287.39

You are to complete the statement of account shown below:

STATEMENT OF ACCOUNT
PRAXIS STATIONERY
45 Jarvis Street, Mereford MR1 2GH

To Rosetti Associates
Date 31 08 20-3

Date	Details	Amount (£)	Balance outstanding (£)
1 August	Invoice 1748		
9 August	Invoice 1778		
10 August	Invoice 1783		
17 August	Credit note 319		
29 August	Cheque		

2.3 Praxis Limited codes all sales invoices with a customer code and a general ledger code.

A selection of the codes used is given below.

Customer	Customer Account Code
Artex Ltd	ART09
Bristol Wholesale	BRI25
Britmore Ltd	BRI45
Coleman Trading	COL10
Coldring Limited	COL12

Item	General Ledger Code
Paper products	GL4002
Pens	GL4003
Storage	GL4008
Printer inks	GL4017
Files	GL4018

Indicate in the table below the appropriate customer and general ledger codes that would be applied to the the following sales invoices:

Product	Customer	General Ledger Code	Customer Code
Copy paper	Britmore Ltd		
Gel pens	Coldring Limited		
Box files	Artex Limited		
Black printer ink	Coleman Trading		
Archive storage boxes	Bristol Wholesale		
Suspension files	Britmore Limited		

2.4   The financial document which is sent by the seller of goods or services and reduces the amount due to the seller is:

	✔
a refund note	
a debit note	
a credit note	

Tick the appropriate box.

2.5   A business sells goods which have a list price of £800. The following discounts are available to the buyer:

- 20% trade discount
- 5% settlement (cash) discount for settlement within 14 days

(a)   The sales invoice should show a VAT amount (at 17.5%) of

	✔
£106.40	
£112.00	
£140.00	

Tick the appropriate box.

(b)   The total price for the goods on the invoice should be:

	✔
£714.40	
£746.40	
£940.00	

Tick the appropriate box.

3 Chapter activities
Accounting for sales and sales returns

3.1 Which one of the following is a financial document?

	✔
sales day book	
sales invoice	
sales ledger account of P Lane	
sales account	

3.2 Which one of the following is in the right order?

	✔
sales returns account; sales ledger control account; customer's account; credit note issued; sales returns day book	
sales returns day book; sales ledger control account; customer's account; sales returns account; credit note issued	
sales returns day book; credit note issued; customer's account; sales returns account; sales ledger control account	
credit note issued; sales returns day book; sales returns account; sales ledger control account; customer's account	

3.3 Which one of the following is entered in the sales returns day book?

	✔
credit note	
purchase order	
statement of account sent to B Roberts, a receivable (debtor)	
sales invoice	

For Activities 3.4 and 3.5:

- work in pounds and pence, where appropriate

- the rate of Value Added Tax is to be calculated at 17.5% (when calculating VAT amounts, you should ignore fractions of a penny, ie round down to a whole penny)

- use a coding system incorporating the following:

sales day book	*– SDB65*	*general ledger account numbers*	
sales returns day book	*– SRDB22*	*sales ledger control account*	*– GL1200*
		sales account	*– GL4100*
sales ledger account numbers		*sales returns account*	*– GL4110*
Dines Stores	*– SL086*	*Value Added Tax account*	*– GL2200*
Meadow Golf Club	*– SL135*		
Raven Retailers Ltd	*– SL170*		
Teme Sports Ltd	*– SL178*		
Wyvern Stores	*– SL195*		

3.4 Pensax Products Limited manufactures and sells sports goods. During November 20-4 the following credit transactions took place:

20-4

3 Nov   Sold goods to Dines Stores £265 + VAT, invoice no 3592 issued

5 Nov   Sold goods to Raven Retailers Limited £335 + VAT, invoice no 3593 issued

6 Nov   Sold goods to Meadow Golf Club £175 + VAT, invoice no 3594 issued

10 Nov   Sold goods to Wyvern Stores £455 + VAT, invoice no 3595 issued

11 Nov   Sold goods to Dines Stores £290 + VAT, invoice no 3596 issued

13 Nov   Sold goods to Teme Sports Limited £315 + VAT, invoice no 3597 issued

17 Nov   Sold goods to Raven Retailers Limited £1,120 + VAT, invoice no 3598 issued

19 Nov   Sold goods to Teme Sports Limited £825 + VAT, invoice no 3599 issued

21 Nov   Sold goods to Dines Stores £354 + VAT, invoice no 3600 issued

24 Nov   Sold goods to Meadow Golf Club £248 + VAT, invoice no 3601 issued

27 Nov   Sold goods to Wyvern Stores £523 + VAT, invoice no 3602 issued

You are to:

(a)   enter the above transactions in Pensax Products' sales day book for November 20-4, using the format shown on the next page

(b)   record the accounting entries in Pensax Products' general ledger and sales ledger. (You will need to retain the ledger accounts for use with Activity 3.5.)

Sales Day Book						SDB65
Date	Details	Invoice number	Reference	Total £	VAT £	Net £

3.5   The following details are the sales returns of Pensax Products Limited for November 20-4. They are to be:

(a)   entered in the sales returns day book for November 20-4, using the format shown on the next page

(b)   recorded in the general ledger and sales ledger (use the ledgers already prepared in the answer to Activity 3.4)

20-4

10 Nov   Dines Stores returns goods £55 + VAT, credit note no 831 issued

14 Nov   Wyvern Stores returns goods £60 + VAT, credit note no 832 issued

19 Nov   Meadow Golf Club returns goods £46 + VAT, credit note no 833 issued

24 Nov   Teme Sports Limited returns goods £127 + VAT, credit note no 834 issued

28 Nov   Dines Stores returns goods £87 + VAT, credit note no 835 issued

Sales Returns Day Book						SRDB22
Date	Details	Credit note number	Reference	Total £	VAT £	Net £

3.6 Sales invoices have been prepared and partially entered in the sales day book, as shown below.

(a) Complete the entries in the sales day book by inserting the appropriate figures for each invoice

(b) Total the last five columns of the sales day book

Sales day book

Date 20XX	Details	Invoice number	Total £	VAT £	Net £	Sales type 1 £	Sales type 2 £
30 June	Olander Ltd	1895		280		1,600	
30 June	Boltz & Co	1896	4,935				4,200
30 June	Ravells	1897	564		480	480	
	Totals						

3.7 You are employed by Beacon Limited as an accounts assistant. The business has a manual accounting system. Double-entry takes place in the general ledger; individual accounts of receivables (debtors) are kept as memorandum accounts in the sales ledger. The VAT rate is 17.5%.

Notes:

- show your answer with a tick, words or figures, as appropriate
- coding is not required

(a)   The following credit transactions all took place on 30 June 20-7 and have been entered into the sales day book as shown below. No entries have yet been made in the ledgers.

Sales day book

Date 20-7	Details	Invoice number	Total £	VAT £	Net £
30 June	Upton Ltd	407	1,974	294	1,680
30 June	Bromyards	408	3,337	497	2,840
30 June	Kempsey & Co	409	4,183	623	3,560
30 June	Fernhill plc	410	2,397	357	2,040
	Totals		11,891	1,771	10,120

What will be the entries in the sales ledger?

Select your account name from the following list: Bromyards, Fernhill plc, Kempsey & Co, Purchases, Purchases ledger control, Purchases returns, Sales, Sales ledger control, Sales returns, Upton Ltd, Value Added Tax.

Sales ledger

Account name	Amount £	Debit ✓	Credit ✓

What will be the entries in the general ledger?

Select your account name from the following list: Purchases, Purchases ledger control, Purchases returns, Sales, Sales ledger control, Sales returns, Value Added Tax.

General ledger

Account name	Amount £	Debit ✓	Credit ✓

(b)   The following credit transactions all took place on 30 June 20-7 and have been entered into the sales returns day book as shown below. No entries have yet been made in the ledgers.

Sales returns day book

Date 20-7	Details	Credit note number	Total £	VAT £	Net £
30 June	Drake & Co	CN 84	329	49	280
30 June	Hanbury Trading	CN 85	987	147	840
	Totals		1,316	196	1,120

What will be the entries in the sales ledger?

Select your account name from the following list: Drake & Co, Hanbury Trading, Purchases, Purchases ledger control, Purchases returns, Sales, Sales ledger control, Sales returns, Value Added Tax.

Sales ledger

Account name	Amount £	Debit ✓	Credit ✓

What will be the entries in the general ledger?

Select your account name from the following list: Purchases, Purchases ledger control, Purchases returns, Sales, Sales ledger control, Sales returns, Value Added Tax.

General ledger

Account name	Amount £	Debit ✓	Credit ✓

Chapter activities

4

Process payments from customers

4.1   A business receiving a remittance advice from a customer will need to check it against the sales documents. Which of the following checks is required?

Choose the correct option.

	✔
Sales documention reference numbers	
The number of the cheque	
Bank account number	
Date of the remittance advice	

4.2   A business receiving a cheque from a customer in payment of an invoice will need to check it to make sure that it is in order. Which of the following list of checks is correct?

Choose the appropriate option.

	✔
Date, signature, bank account number	
Date, signature, bank sort code	
Same amount in words and figures, in date, signature of customer	
Same amount in words and figures, in date, invoice number	

Task 4.3

The account shown below is in the sales ledger of Johnston & Co. Also shown below is a BACS remittance advice received from R Romero at the end of August.

R Romero					
Date 20XX	Details	Amount £	Date 20XX	Details	Amount £
1 Aug	Balance b/f	2,790	2 Aug	Bank	2,790
10 Aug	Sales invoice 392	690	26 June	Sales returns credit note 295	90
25 Aug	Sales Invoice 417	1,100			

R Romero

BACS REMITTANCE ADVICE

To: Johnston & Co   Date: 28 August 20XX

The following payment will reach your bank account within 3 working days.

Invoice number	Credit note number	Amount £
392		590
417		1,100
Total amount paid		1,690

You are required to check the remittance advice against the sales ledger account.

State two discrepancies you can identify:

(a)

(b)

5 Chapter activities
Process documents from suppliers

5.1 When a credit note is received by the buyer in respect of faulty goods returned by the buyer, it should be checked against the details on the:

	✔
invoice	
delivery note	
remittance advice	

5.2 A business will use supplier codes to refer to accounts in:

	✔
the general ledger	
the sales ledger	
the purchases ledger	

Tick the appropriate box.

5.3 A business will use general ledger codes to refer to accounts for:

	✔
purchases	
suppliers	
customers	

Tick the appropriate box.

5.4 A supply of office chairs has been delivered to Praxis Stationery. Praxis Stationery completes a Goods Received Note as shown below.

Examine the note and answer the questions below by selecting the correct words from the following list:

Praxis Stationery	**2 chairs missing**	**2 chairs damaged**	**purchases day book**
credit note	**Helicon Furniture**	**debit note**	**sales day book**
sales ledger	**returns note**	**refund note**	**purchase ledeger**

GOODS RECEIVED NOTE
PRAXIS STATIONERY

GRN no.   302

supplier   Helicon Furniture

date   4 December 20-4

order ref.	quantity	description
8246	10	Office chairs (Code Typ72652)

received by...*D Nutt*..checked by...*N Mason*..................

condition of goods   condition - *good (8 chairs)*
damages - *2 chairs damaged*
shortages *none*

(a) Who has supplied the chairs?

(b) What is the problem with the consignment?

(c) What document would be issued by the supplier to adjust the account of Praxis Stationery?

(d) Where in the supplier's accounting records would the account of Praxis Stationery be maintained?

5.5   A supply of office chairs has been delivered to Praxis Stationery by Firth Furniture. The purchase order sent from Praxis Stationery, and the invoice from Firth Furniture, are shown below.

PURCHASE ORDER
PRAXIS STATIONERY

No 1066
Date 10 08 20-3

45 Jarvis Street, Mereford MR1 2GH

To: Firth Furniture

Please supply 12 Executive office chairs (product code EXCH45)

Purchase price: £150 each, plus VAT @ 17.5%.

Discount: less 20% trade discount, as agreed

INVOICE
FIRTH FURNITURE
17 Chippendale Street
Lesspool LP1 5HG
VAT Reg 171 7326 11

To:
Praxis Stationery
45 Jarvis Street, Mereford MR1 2GH

Date 11 08 20-3
No. 6518

Account PS6232

Quantity	Product code	Price (£)	Total (£)	Net (£)	VAT (£)	Total (£)
12	EXCH45	150.00	1,800.00	1,620.00	283.50	1,903.50

Check the invoice against the purchase order and answer the following questions:

Has the correct purchase price of the chairs been charged? Yes or No?	
Has the correct discount been applied? Yes or No?	
What would be the VAT amount charged if the invoice was correct?	£
What would be the total amount charged if the invoice was correct?	£

5.6 A supply of office desks has been delivered to Praxis Stationery by Firth Furniture. The purchase order sent from Praxis Stationery, and the delivery note from Firth Furniture, are shown below.

PURCHASE ORDER
PRAXIS STATIONERY

No 1261
Date 05 09 20-3

45 Jarvis Street, Mereford MR1 2GH

To: Firth Furniture

Please supply 4 oak finish office tables (product code OTT28)

Purchase price: £80 each, plus VAT @ 17.5%.

Discount: less 20% trade discount, as agreed.

DELIVERY NOTE
FIRTH FURNITURE
17 Chippendale Street
Lesspool LP1 5HG
VAT Reg 171 7326 11

To:
Praxis Stationery
45 Jarvis Street, Mereford MR1 2GH

Date 10 09 20-3
No. 6610
Account PS6232

Quantity	Product code	Description
5	OTT28	Office tables, teak finish (product code OTT28) @ £80 each, less trade discount @ 20%, plus VAT @ 17.5%.

Check the delivery note against the purchase order and answer the following questions:

Has the correct number of tables been supplied? Yes or No?	
Has the correct type of table been supplied? Yes or No?	
What will be the total of the invoice on the basis of the details on the delivery note?	£
If a credit note were issued, what would be the total, including VAT?	£

Chapter activities

6 Accounting for purchases and purchases returns

6.1 Which one of the following is a financial document?

	✔
purchases invoice	
statement of account sent by T Lewis, a payable (creditor)	
purchases day book	
purchases ledger control account	

6.2 Which one of the following is in the right order?

	✔
purchases day book; purchases ledger control account; invoice received; purchases account; supplier's account	
purchases account; supplier's account; purchases ledger control account; purchases day book; invoice received	
invoice received; purchases day book; purchases account; purchases ledger control account; supplier's account	
invoice received; purchases account; purchases ledger control account; supplier's account; purchases day book	

6.3 Which one of the following shows the correct general ledger entries to record the purchase of goods for resale on credit?

	✔
debit purchases ledger control; debit VAT; credit purchases	
debit purchases ledger control; credit purchases; credit VAT	
debit purchases; debit VAT; credit purchases ledger control	
debit purchases; credit purchases ledger control; credit VAT	

For Activities 6.4 and 6.5:

- work in pounds and pence, where appropriate

- the rate of Value Added Tax is to be calculated at 17.5% (when calculating VAT amounts, you should ignore fractions of a penny, ie round down to a whole penny)

- use a coding system incorporating the following:

purchases day book	*– PDB55*		
purchases returns day book	*– PRDB14*	*general ledger account numbers*	
		purchases ledger control account	*– GL2350*
purchases ledger account numbers		*purchases account*	*– GL5100*
S Burston	*– PL530*	*purchases returns account*	*– GL5110*
Iley Supplies Ltd	*– PL605*	*Value Added Tax account*	*– GL2200*
Malvern Manufacturing	*– PL625*		
SG Enterprises	*– PL720*		

6.4 Wyvern Products Limited manufactures and sells garden furniture. During May 20-2 the following credit transactions took place:

20-2

3 May Purchased goods from Malvern Manufacturing £170 + VAT, invoice no 7321

9 May Purchased goods from S Burston £265 + VAT, invoice no SB745

12 May Purchased goods from Iley Supplies Ltd £450 + VAT, invoice no 4721

18 May Purchased goods from SG Enterprises £825 + VAT, invoice no 3947

23 May Purchased goods from S Burston £427 + VAT, invoice no SB773

30 May Purchased goods from Malvern Manufacturing £364 + VAT, invoice no 7408

You are to:

(a) enter the above transactions in Wyvern Products Limited's purchases day book for May 20-2, using the format shown on the next page

(b) record the accounting entries in Wyvern Products Limited's general ledger and purchases ledger. (You will need to retain the ledger accounts for use with Activity 6.5)

Purchases Day Book						PDB55
Date	Details	Invoice number	Reference	Total £	VAT £	Net £

6.5 The following are the purchases returns of Wyvern Products Limited for May 20-2. They are to be:

(a) entered in the purchases returns day book for May 20-2, using the format shown on the next page

(b) recorded in the general ledger and sales ledger (use the ledgers already prepared in the answer to Activity 6.4)

20-2

11 May   Returned goods to Malvern Manufacturing £70 + VAT, credit note no CN345 received

17 May   Returned goods to Iley Supplies Ltd £85 + VAT, credit note no CN241 received

24 May   Returned goods to SG Enterprises £25 + VAT, credit note no 85 received

31 May   Returned goods to S Burston £55 + VAT, credit note no SB95 received

		Purchases Returns Day Book				PRDB14
Date	Details	Credit note number	Reference	Total £	VAT £	Net £

6.6 Purchases invoices have been prepared and partially entered in the purchases day book, as shown below.

(a) Complete the entries in the purchases day book by inserting the appropriate figures for each invoice

(b) Total the last five columns of the purchases day book

Purchases day book

Date 20XX	Details	Invoice number	Total £	VAT £	Net £	Purchases type 1 £	Purchases type 2 £
30 June	King & Co	K641	1,974		1,680		1,680
30 June	Rossingtons	2129		448		2,560	
30 June	Moniz Ltd	M/149	2,162				1,840
	Totals						

6.7 You are employed by Churchtown Limited as an accounts assistant. The business has a manual accounting system. Double-entry takes place in the general ledger; individual accounts of payables (creditors) are kept as memorandum accounts in the purchases ledger. The VAT rate is 17.5%.

Notes:

- show your answer with a tick, words or figures, as appropriate
- coding is not required

(a) The following credit transactions all took place on 30 June 20-8 and have been entered into the purchases day book as shown below. No entries have yet been made in the ledgers.

Purchases day book

Date 20-8	Details	Invoice number	Total £	VAT £	Net £
30 June	H & L Ltd	5986	6,392	952	5,440
30 June	Sperrin & Co	P864	2,162	322	1,840
30 June	Hickmores	H591	4,512	672	3,840
30 June	Marklew plc	6417	1,081	161	920
	Totals		14,147	2,107	12,040

What will be the entries in the purchases ledger?

Select your account name from the following list: H & L Ltd, Hickmores, Marklew plc, Purchases, Purchases ledger control, Purchases returns, Sales, Sales ledger control, Sales returns, Sperrin & Co, Value Added Tax.

Purchases ledger

Account name	Amount £	Debit ✓	Credit ✓

What will be the entries in the general ledger?

Select your account name from the following list: Purchases, Purchases ledger control, Purchases returns, Sales, Sales ledger control, Sales returns, Value Added Tax.

General ledger

Account name	Amount £	Debit ✓	Credit ✓

(b) The following credit transactions all took place on 30 June 20-8 and have been entered into the purchases returns day book as shown below. No entries have yet been made in the ledgers.

Purchases returns day book

Date 20-8	Details	Credit note number	Total £	VAT £	Net £
30 June	Marcer Transport	564	611	91	520
30 June	Schuller Ltd	CN28	423	63	360
	Totals		1,034	154	880

What will be the entries in the purchases ledger?

Select your account name from the following list: Marcer Transport, Purchases, Purchases ledger control, Purchases returns, Sales, Sales ledger control, Sales returns, Schuller Ltd, Value Added Tax.

Purchases ledger

Account name	Amount £	Debit ✓	Credit ✓

What will be the entries in the general ledger?

Select your account name from the following list: Purchases, Purchases ledger control, Purchases returns, Sales, Sales ledger control, Sales returns, Value Added Tax.

General ledger

Account name	Amount £	Debit ✓	Credit ✓

7   Chapter activities
Prepare payments to suppliers

7.1   If a supplier duplicates an invoice for goods ordered, the likely effect will be:

	✔
an increase in the total amount owing shown on the statement of account	
a decrease in the total amount owing shown on the statement of account	
no effect at all	

7.2   A remittance advice is likely to show details of the following financial documents issued:

	✔
purchase invoices, purchase credit notes, goods received notes	
purchase invoices, purchase credit notes, cheques issued	
purchase invoices, purchase credit notes, total amount owing	

Tick the appropriate box.

7.3   The purchase ledger account of a supplier shows a purchase invoice which is not shown on the supplier's statement of account. This:

	✔
can be adjusted by asking the supplier to issue a credit note	
will reduce the total amount shown as owing on the statement of account	
will increase the total amount shown as owing on the statement of account	

Tick the appropriate box.

7.4 Shown below is a statement of account received from Masters Supplies, a credit supplier, and the supplier's account as shown in the purchases ledger of Broadfield Traders.

Masters Supplies

21 HighStreet, East Mereford, MR7 9HJ

To: Broadfield Traders

Unit 18 Elgar Estate

Mereford, MR2 5FG   **STATEMENT OF ACCOUNT**

Date 20XX	Invoice Number	Details	Invoice Amount £	Cheque Amount £	Balance £
1 May	699	Goods	2,000		2,000
5 May	712	Goods	1,100		3,100
9 May	731	Goods	750		3,850
28 May	790	Goods	1,360		5,210
1 June	-	Cheque		3,850	1,360

		Masters Supplies			
Date 20XX	Details	Amount £	Date 20XX	Details	Amount £
1 June	Bank	3,850	1 May	Purchases	2,000
28 June	Bank	1,000	8 May	Purchases	1,100
			10 May	Purchases	750

(a) Which item is missing from the statement of account from Masters Supplies? *Select your answer from the following list:*

Invoice 600, Invoice 712, Invoice 731, Invoice 790, Cheque for £3,850, Cheque for £1,000

(b) Which item is missing from the supplier account in Broadfield Traders' purchases ledger? *Select your answer from the following list:*

Invoice 699, Invoice 712, Invoice 731, Invoice 790, Cheque for £3,850, Cheque for £1,000

(c) Assuming any differences between the statement of account from Masters Supplies and the supplier account in Broadfield Traders' purchases ledger are simply due to omission errors, what is the amount owing to Masters Supplies?

£

7.5 Mereford Traders sends BACS remittance advice notes to suppliers on the last day of the month following the month of invoice. Mereford Traders banks with National Bank plc and A Strauss & Co banks with Mercia Bank plc. Below is an uncompleted BACS remittance advice and an extract from Mereford Trader's purchases ledger.

Mereford Traders
45 College Street
Mereford, MR3 4GT
BACS REMITTANCE ADVICE

To: Date:

The following payment will reach your bank account within 3 working days.

Invoice number	Credit note number	Amount £
	Total amount paid	

A Strauss & Co					
Date	Details	Amount	Date	Details	Amount
20XX		£	20XX		£
3 Feb	Purchases returns credit note CN101	400	15 Feb	Purchases Invoice 2250	1,750
20 Mar	Purchases returns credit note CN105	300	12 Mar	Purchases Invoice 2461	2,340
30 Mar	Bank	1,350	29 Mar	Purchases Invoice 2479	1,600
			10 Apl	Purchases Invoice 2499	2,107

(a) the BACS remittance advice will be sent . . . .

	✔
with a cheque to Mereford Traders	
without a cheque to A Strauss & Co	
to Mercia Bank plc with a cheque	
to Mercia Bank plc without a cheque	

Select the correct option.

(b)   What will be the date shown on the BACS remittance advice?

✔

28 February	
31 March	
30 April	
31 May	

Select the correct option

(c)   What will be the items shown on the BACS remittance advice?

✔

Invoice 2250, Invoice 2461, invoice 2479, invoice 2687	
Invoice 2461, invoice 2479, credit note CN105	
Invoice 2250, Invoice 2461, invoice 2479, credit note CN101	
Invoice 2250, Invoice 2461, credit note CN101, credit note CN105	

Select the correct option

(d)   The amount of the remittance advice will be . . . .

✔

£3,390	
£4,990	
£3,640	
£5,390	

Select the correct option

8 Chapter activities
Cash book

8.1 A business has made a cash purchase for £200 plus VAT at 17.5%. Which one of the following is correct double-entry book-keeping to record the purchase?

	✔
debit bank £200; debit VAT £35; credit purchases £235	
debit bank £235; credit purchases £200; credit VAT £35	
debit purchases £235; debit VAT £35; credit bank £270	
debit purchases £200; debit VAT £35; credit bank £235	

8.2 The discount allowed column of the cash book is totalled at regular intervals and transferred to:

	✔
the credit side of discount allowed account	
the debit side of discount allowed account	
the debit side of sales account	
the credit side of sales account	

8.3 The VAT column on the payments side of the cash book is totalled at regular intervals and transferred to:

	✔
the debit side of general expenses account	
the debit side of VAT account	
the credit side of purchases account	
the credit side of VAT account	

8.4 The following transactions all took place on 30 June 20-4 and have been entered into the cash book of Rafe Sadler, as shown below. No entries have yet been made in the ledgers.

Dr					Cash Book		CB73	Cr
Date	Details	Discounts	Bank	Date	Details		VAT	Bank
20-4		£	£	20-4			£	£
30 Jun	Balance b/f		3,840	30 Jun	Wages			1,175
30 Jun	Smithsons Ltd (receivable)	100	2,750	30 Jun	Rent			1,200
				30 Jun	Stationery		105	705
				30 Jun	Balance c/d			3,510
		100	6,590				105	6,590
1 Jul	Balance b/d		3,510					

(a) What will be the entries in the sales ledger?

Select your account name from the following list: Balance b/f, Bank, Discounts allowed, Discounts received, Purchases ledger control, Sales Ledger control, Smithsons Ltd.

Sales ledger

Account name	Amount £	Debit ✓	Credit ✓

(b) What will be the entries in the general ledger?

Select your account name from the following list: Balance b/f, Bank, Discounts allowed, Discounts received, Purchases ledger control, Rent, Sales Ledger control, Stationery, Smithsons Ltd, Value Added Tax, Wages.

General ledger

Account name	Amount £	Debit ✓	Credit ✓

8.5 The following cash book shows a number of transactions of Wentworths which all took place on 30 September 20-1:

Dr							Cash Book			CB68		Cr
Date	Details	Ref	Discounts	VAT	Bank	Date	Details	Ref	Discounts	VAT	Bank
			£	£	£	20-1			£	£	£
20-1					3,045	30 Sep	Nelson Stores				
30 Sep	Balance b/f			77	517		(payable)		30		1,940
30 Sep	Cash sales					30 Sep	Cash purchases			28	188
30 Sep	Albany Ltd				1,580	30 Sep	General expenses			112	752
	(receivable)		25			30 Sep	Wages				1,254
30 Sep	Balance c/d				402	30 Sep	Office equipment			210	1,410
			25	77	5,544				30	350	5,544
						1 Oct	Balance b/d				402

(a) The balance brought forward of £3,045 on 30 September shows that, according to the cash book, the business has money in the bank. True or false?

(b) The balance brought down of £402 on 1 October shows that, according to the cash book, the business has money in the bank. True or false?

(c) You are to transfer the data from the cash book into the general ledger of Wentworths. Note that a bank control account is not required.

(d) Show the entries in the sales ledger and purchases ledger of Wentworths.

8.6   The following transactions all took place on 30 June and have been entered in the debit side of the cash book of Jane Martin, as shown below. No entries have yet been made in the ledgers.

Cash book – Debit side

Date 20XX	Details	Discounts £	Bank £
30 June	Balance b/f		2,076
30 June	Boscawen Ltd	45	1,540

(a)   What will be the entries in the sales ledger?

Select your account name from the following list: Balance b/f, Bank, Boscawen Ltd, Discounts allowed, Discounts received, Purchases ledger control, Sales ledger control.

Sales ledger

Account name	Amount £	Debit ✓	Credit ✓

(b)   What will be the entries in the general ledger?

Select your account name from the following list: Balance b/f, Bank, Boscawen Ltd, Discounts allowed, Discounts received, Purchases ledger control, Sales ledger control.

General ledger

Account name	Amount £	Debit ✓	Credit ✓

The following transactions all took place on 30 June and have been entered in the credit side of the cash book of Jane Martin, as shown below. No entries have yet been made in the ledgers.

Cash book – Credit side

Date 20XX	Details	VAT £	Bank £
30 June	Wages		1,265
30 June	Office equipment	287	1,927

(c)   What will be the entries in the general ledger?

Select your account name from the following list: Bank, Office equipment, Purchases ledger control, Sales ledger control, Value Added Tax, Wages.

General ledger

Account name	Amount £	Debit ✓	Credit ✓

9 Chapter activities
Petty cash book

9.1   The imprest system for petty cash means that:

	✔
petty cash payments up to a stated amount can be authorised by the petty cashier	
petty cash vouchers must have relevant documentation attached	
the petty cash float is restored to the same amount for the beginning of each week or month	
petty cash vouchers are numbered and the number is recorded in the petty cash book	

9.2   A petty cash control account has a balance b/d of £150 at the beginning of a month. During the month, payments are made from petty cash which total £108. Which one of the following transactions will restore the balance of petty cash control account to £150?

	✔
debit bank £150; credit petty cash control £150	
debit petty cash control £108; credit bank £108	
debit petty cash control £42; credit bank £42	
debit bank £108; credit petty cash control £108	

9.3   Show whether the following statements are true or false.

Statement	True ✔	False ✔
payments are recorded on the debit side of petty cash book		
a petty cash book may combine the roles of a book of prime entry and double-entry book-keeping		
petty cash vouchers are authorised for payment by the petty cashier		
the totals of the petty cash analysis columns are transferred to general ledger where they are debited to the appropriate expense account		

9.4 The petty cashier of the business where you work tops up the petty cash at the end of the month with £110 withdrawn from the bank.

What will be the entries in the general ledger?

Select your account name from the following list: Bank, Cash, Petty cash book, Purchases, Purchases ledger control, Sales, Sales ledger control, Value Added Tax.

General ledger

Account name	Amount £	Debit ✓	Credit ✓

9.5   Wyvern Property maintains a petty cash book as both a book of prime entry and part of the double-entry accounting system. The following transactions all took place on 30 June and have been entered in the petty cash book as shown below. No entries have yet been made in the general ledger.

Petty cash book

Date 20XX	Details	Amount £	Date 20XX	Details	Amount £	VAT £	Postage £	Travel expenses £	Stationery £
30 Jun	Balance b/f	68.00	30 Jun	Taxi	14.57	2.17		12.40	
30 Jun	Bank	57.00	30 Jun	Copy paper	18.33	2.73			15.60
			30 Jun	Post office	11.50		11.50		
			30 Jun	Rail fare	22.35			22.35	
				Balance c/d	58.25				
		125.00			125.00	4.90	11.50	34.75	15.60

What will be the entries in the general ledger?

Select your account name from the following list: Balance b/f, Balance c/d, Bank, Copy paper, Petty cash book, Postage, Post office, Rail fare, Stationery, Taxi, Travel expenses, Value Added Tax.

General ledger

Account name	Amount £	Debit ✓	Credit ✓

9.6 The following petty cash book shows a number of transactions of Elliotts Limited for July 20-6. The petty cash book is kept solely as a book of prime entry.

					Petty Cash Book						**PCB35**
Receipts	Date	Details	Voucher	Total			Analysis columns			
			number	payment	VAT	Travel	Postages	Stationery	Meals	Ledger
£	20-6			£	£	£	£	£	£	£
200.00	1 Jul	Balance b/f								
	6 Jul	Post office	104	11.55			11.55			
	9 Jul	Rail fare	105	17.60		17.60				
	11 Jul	Envelopes	106	9.40	1.40			8.00		
	12 Jul	Meal allowance	107	10.00					10.00	
6.25	14 Jul	T Irwin (postage)	582							
	19 Jul	Taxi	108	9.87	1.47	8.40				
	22 Jul	J Clarke (PL)	109	18.25						18.25
	25 Jul	Marker pens	110	6.11	0.91			5.20		
				82.78	3.78	26.00	11.55	13.20	10.00	18.25
76.53	31 Jul	Bank								
	31 Jul	Balance c/d		200.00						
282.78				282.78						
200.00	1 Aug	Balance b/d								

(a) You are to transfer the data from the petty cash book into the general ledger accounts (including cash book) as at 31 July 20-6. Note that a petty cash control is required.

(b) Show the entry that will be recorded in purchases ledger as at 31 July 20-6.

10 Chapter activities

Balancing accounts, the accounting equation, capital and revenue

10.1 The following three accounts are in the general ledger at the close of day on 30 June.

(a)   **Insert the balance carried down together with date and details**

(b)   **Insert the totals**

(c)   **Insert the balance brought down together with date and details**

For each account select your account name from the following list: Balance b/f, Balance c/d, Bank, Closing balance, Opening balance, Purchases ledger control

Vehicle expenses

Date 20XX	Details	Amount £	Date 20XX	Details	Amount £
01 Jun	Balance b/f	2,055			
23 Jun	Bank	220			
	Total			Total	

Discounts received

Date 20XX	Details	Amount £	Date 20XX	Details	Amount £
			01 Jun	Balance b/f	725
			30 Jun	Purchases ledger control	115
	Total			Total	

Commission received

Date 20XX	Details	Amount £	Date 20XX	Details	Amount £
			01 Jun	Balance b/f	2,680
			19 Jun	Bank	465
	Total			Total	

10.2   Financial accounting is based upon the accounting equation.

   (a)   **Show whether the following statements are true or false.**

Statement	True ✓	False ✓
Liabilities equals capital plus assets		
Assets equals liabilities minus capital		
Capital equals assets minus liabilities		

   (b)   **Classify each of the following items as an asset or a liability.**

Item	Asset ✓	Liability ✓
Vehicles		
Bank loan		
Money owing by receivables (debtors)		
Inventory (stock)		
Cash		
VAT owing to HM Revenue and Customs		

10.3   Fill in the missing figures:

Assets	Liabilities	Capital
£	£	£
50,000	0	....
40,000	10,000	....
55,200	....	30,250
....	18,220	40,760
40,320	15,980	....
....	24,760	48,590

10.4 The table below sets out account balances from the books of a business. The opening capital is £20,000 which has been paid into the business bank account.

The columns (a) to (f) show the account balances resulting from a series of financial transactions that have taken place over time.

You are to compare each set of adjacent columns, ie (a) with (b), (b) with (c), and so on and state, with figures, what financial transactions have taken place in each case. The first has been completed for you.

Ignore VAT.

	(a)	(b)	(c)	(d)	(e)	(f)
	£	£	£	£	£	£
Assets						
Vehicles	–	10,000	10,000	10,000	18,000	18,000
Inventory (stock)	–	–	6,000	9,000	9,000	9,000
Bank	20,000	10,000	4,000	4,000	1,000	11,000
Liabilities						
Loan	–	–	–	–	5,000	5,000
Payables (creditors)	–	–	–	3,000	3,000	3,000
Capital	20,000	20,000	20,000	20,000	20,000	30,000

Answer (a) - (b): Vehicles have been bought for £10,000, paid from the bank.

10.5   It is important to understand the difference between capital expenditure, revenue expenditure, capital income and revenue income.

Select one option in each instance below to show whether the item will be capital expenditure, revenue expenditure, capital income or revenue income.

Item	Capital expenditure ✓	Revenue expenditure ✓	Capital income ✓	Revenue income ✓
Purchase of vehicles				
Fuel for vehicles				
Discounts received				
Receipts from sale of office equipment				
Redecoration of property				
Extension to property				
Receipts from sale of goods to credit customers				
Delivery cost of new machine				
Increase in owner's capital				
Repairs to vehicles				

11   Chapter activities
The initial trial balance

11.1   Which one of the following accounts always has a credit balance?

	✔
drawings account	
sales returns account	
sales account	
office equipment account	

11.2   Which one of the following accounts always has a debit balance?

	✔
purchases returns account	
sales ledger control account	
capital account	
loan account	

11.3 Prepare the initial trial balance of Kate Trelawney as at 31 March 20-2. She has omitted to open a capital account. You are to fill in the missing figure in order to balance the trial balance.

	£
Bank loan	3,650
Purchases	23,745
Vehicle	9,500
Sales	65,034
Bank (debit balance)	2,162
Discount allowed	317
Purchases returns	855
Sales ledger control	7,045
Office equipment	5,450
Inventory (stock) at 1 April 20-1	4,381
Sales returns	1,624
Purchases ledger control	4,736
Expenses	32,598
Discount received	494
Capital	?

11.4 You work as an accounts assistant for Wyvern Trading. The accounts supervisor has asked you to work on preparing an initial trial balance as at 31 December 20-8. The supervisor has given you the following list of balances to be transferred to the trial balance.

You are to place the figures in the debit or credit column, as appropriate, and to total each column.

Account name	Amount £	Debit £	Credit £
Bank overdraft	4,293		
Loan from bank	12,500		
Vehicles	25,500		
Inventory (stock)	10,417		
Petty cash control	68		
Capital	25,794		
VAT owing to HM Revenue and Customs	1,496		
Purchases ledger control	12,794		
Purchases	104,763		
Purchases returns	2,681		
Sales ledger control	28,354		
Sales	184,267		
Sales returns	4,098		
Discount allowed	1,312		
Discount received	1,784		
Wages	35,961		
Telephone	3,474		
Advertising	5,921		
Insurance	3,084		
Heating and lighting	2,477		
Rent and rates	3,672		
Postages	876		
Miscellaneous expenses	545		
Drawings	15,087		
Totals	–		

11.5 You work as an accounts assistant for Highley Limited. The accounts supervisor has asked you to work on preparing an initial trial balance as at 30 June 20-1. The supervisor has given you the following list of balances to be transferred to the trial balance.

You are to place the figures in the debit or credit column, as appropriate, and to total each column.

Account name	Amount £	Debit £	Credit £
Sales	262,394		
Sales returns	2,107		
Sales ledger control	33,844		
Purchases	157,988		
Purchases returns	1,745		
Purchases ledger control	17,311		
Discount received	1,297		
Discount allowed	845		
Rent and rates	5,941		
Advertising	6,088		
Insurance	3,176		
Wages	48,954		
Heating and lighting	4,266		
Postages and telephone	2,107		
Miscellaneous expenses	632		
Vehicles	28,400		
Capital	48,756		
Drawings	19,354		
Office equipment	10,500		
Inventory (stock)	16,246		
Petty cash control	150		
Bank (debit balance)	3,096		
VAT owing to HM Revenue and Customs	3,721		
Loan from bank	8,470		
Totals	–		

Answers to chapter activities

1
Chapter activities – answers
Introduction to the accounting system

1.1 Cash sale

1.2 The first place an entry is recorded in the accounting records

1.3 Cash and credit and other financial transactions

1.4 Customers who buy goods and services on a credit basis

1.5 A *trial balance* sets out in two columns the balances of the *ledger accounts* of a business. The *totals* of the two columns should *agree*. The debit column includes the accounts of *receivables* and the credit column includes the accounts of *payables.* This provides the *managers* of a business with important and useful financial information.

2
Chapter activities – answers
Financial documents for sales

2.1 **(a)**

INVOICE   **No** 1689

PRAXIS STATIONERY   **Date** 09 07 20-3
45 Jarvis Street
Mereford MR1 2GH
VAT Reg 831 8627 06

To
Dover Designs
68 Whitecliff Street, Granstow, GR3 7GH   Customer code   DO109

                                             Delivery note no 246

Quantity	Product code	Unit price (£)	Total (£)	Net (£)	VAT (£)	Total (£)
100	BX100	4.00	400.00	320.00	54.88	374.88

(b)   £374.88

2.2

STATEMENT OF ACCOUNT			To Rosetti Associates
PRAXIS STATIONERY 45 Jarvis Street, Mereford MR1 2GH			**Date** 31 08 20-3

Date	Details	Amount (£)	Balance outstanding (£)
1 August	Invoice 1748	4,567.89	4,567.89
9 August	Invoice 1778	2,457.60	7,025.49
10 August	Invoice 1783	4,678.30	11,703.79
17 August	Credit note 319	280.50	11,423.29
29 August	Cheque	4,287.39	7,135.90

2.3

Product	Customer	General Ledger Code	Customer Code
Copy paper	Britmore Ltd	GL4002	BRI45
Gel pens	Coldring Limited	GL4003	COL12
Box files	Artex Limited	GI 4018	ART09
Black printer ink	Coleman Trading	GL4017	COL10
Archive storage boxes	Bristol Wholesale	GL4008	BRI25
Suspension files	Britmore Limited	GL4018	BRI45

2.4   a credit note

2.5   **(a)**   £106.40
         (b)   £746.40

3 Chapter activities – answers
Accounting for sales and sales returns

3.1 sales invoice

3.2 credit note issued; sales returns day book; sales returns account; sales ledger control account; customer's account

3.3 credit note

3.4 (a)

Sales Day Book						SDB65
Date	Details	Invoice number	Reference	Total	VAT	Net
20-4				£	£	£
3 Nov	Dines Stores	3592	SL086	311.37	46.37	265.00
5 Nov	Raven Retailers Ltd	3593	SL170	393.62	58.62	335.00
6 Nov	Meadow Golf Club	3594	SL135	205.62	30.62	175.00
10 Nov	Wyvern Stores	3595	SL195	534.62	79.62	455.00
11 Nov	Dines Stores	3596	SL086	340.75	50.75	290.00
13 Nov	Teme Sports Ltd	3597	SL178	370.12	55.12	315.00
17 Nov	Raven Retailers Ltd	3598	SL170	1,316.00	196.00	1,120.00
19 Nov	Teme Sports Ltd	3599	SL178	969.37	144.37	825.00
21 Nov	Dines Stores	3600	SL086	415.95	61.95	354.00
24 Nov	Meadow Golf Club	3601	SL135	291.40	43.40	248.00
27 Nov	Wyvern Stores	3602	SL195	614.52	91.52	523.00
30 Nov	Totals for month			5,763.34	858.34	4,905.00
				GL1200	GL2200	GL4100

878

9889999

889999999

9

(b)

GENERAL LEDGER

Dr **Sales Ledger Control Account** (GL1200) Cr

20-4			£	20-4		£
30 Nov	Sales Day Book	SDB65	5,763.34			

Dr **Value Added Tax Account** (GL2200) Cr

20-4			£	20-4		£
				30 Nov Sales Day Book SDB65		858.34

Dr **Sales Account** (GL4100) Cr

20-4			£	20-4		£
				30 Nov Sales Day Book SDB65		4,905.00

SALES LEDGER

Dr **Dines Stores** (SL086) Cr

20-4			£	20-4	£
3 Nov	Sales	SDB65	311.37		
11 Nov	Sales	SDB65	340.75		
21 Nov	Sales	SDB65	415.95		

Dr **Meadow Golf Club** (SL135) Cr

20-4			£	20-4	£
6 Nov	Sales	SDB65	205.62		
24 Nov	Sales	SDB65	291.40		

Dr **Raven Retailers Limited** (SL170) Cr

20-4			£	20-4	£
5 Nov	Sales	SDB65	393.62		
17 Nov	Sales	SDB65	1,316.00		

Dr **Teme Sports Limited** (SL178) Cr

20-4			£	20-4	£
13 Nov	Sales	SDB65	370.12		
19 Nov	Sales	SDB65	969.37		

Dr **Wyvern Stores** (SL195) Cr

20-4			£	20-4	£
10 Nov	Sales	SDB65	534.62		
27 Nov	Sales	SDB65	614.52		

3.5   (a)

Sales Returns Day Book						SRDB22
Date	Details	Credit note number	Reference	Total	VAT	Net
20-4				£	£	£
10 Nov	Dines Stores	831	SL086	64.62	9.62	55.00
14 Nov	Wyvern Stores	832	SL195	70.50	10.50	60.00
19 Nov	Meadow Golf Club	833	SL135	54.05	8.05	46.00
24 Nov	Teme Sports Ltd	834	SL178	149.22	22.22	127.00
28 Nov	Dines Stores	835	SL086	102.22	15.22	87.00
30 Nov	Totals for month			440.61	65.61	375.00
				GL1200	GL2200	GL4110

(b)   **GENERAL LEDGER**

Dr   **Sales Ledger Control Account** (GL1200)   Cr

20-4		£	20-4			£
30 Nov Sales Day Book	SDB65	5,763.34	30 Nov Sales Returns Day Book	SRDB22	440.61	

Dr   **Value Added Tax Account** (GL2200)   Cr

20-4		£	20-4			£
30 Nov Sales Returns Day Book	SRDB22	65.61	30 Nov Sales Day Book	SDB65	858.34	

Dr   **Sales Returns Account** (GL4110)   Cr

20-4		£	20-4	£
30 Nov Sales Returns Day Book	SRDB22	375.00		

SALES LEDGER

Dr	**Dines Stores** (SL086)				Cr
20-4		£	20-4		£
3 Nov Sales	SDB65	311.37	10 Nov Sales Returns	SRDB22	64.62
11 Nov Sales	SDB65	340.75	28 Nov Sales Returns	SRDB22	102.22
21 Nov Sales	SDB65	415.95			

Dr	**Meadow Golf Club** (SL135)				Cr
20-4		£	20-4		£
6 Nov Sales	SDB65	205.62	19 Nov Sales Returns	SRDB22	54.05
24 Nov Sales	SDB65	291.40			

Dr	**Teme Sports Limited** (SL178)				Cr
20-4		£	20-4		£
13 Nov Sales	SDB65	370.12	24 Nov Sales Returns	SRDB22	149.22
19 Nov Sales	SDB65	969.37			

Dr	**Wyvern Stores** (SL195)				Cr
20-4		£	20-4		£
10 Nov Sales	SDB65	534.62	14 Nov Sales Returns	SRDB22	70.50
27 Nov Sales	SDB65	614.52			

3.6   (a) & (b)

Sales day book

Date 20XX	Details	Invoice number	Total £	VAT £	Net £	Sales type 1 £	Sales type 2 £
30 June	Olander Ltd	1895	1,880	280	1,600	1,600	
30 June	Boltz & Co	1896	4,935	735	4,200		4,200
30 June	Ravells	1897	564	84	480	480	
	Totals		7,379	1,099	6,280	2,080	4,200

3.7   (a)

Sales ledger

Account name	Amount £	Debit ✓	Credit ✓
Upton Ltd	1,974	✓	
Bromyards	3,337	✓	
Kempsey & Co	4,183	✓	
Fernhill plc	2,397	✓	

General ledger

Account name	Amount £	Debit ✓	Credit ✓
Sales	10,120		✓
Value Added Tax	1,771		✓
Sales ledger control	11,891	✓	

(b)

Sales ledger

Account name	Amount £	Debit ✓	Credit ✓
Drake & Co	329		✓
Hanbury Trading	987		✓

General ledger

Account name	Amount £	Debit ✓	Credit ✓
Sales returns	1,120	✓	
Value Added Tax	196	✓	
Sales ledger control	1,316		✓

4 Chapter activities – answers
Process payments from customers

4.1   Sales documention reference numbers

4.2   Same amount in words and figures, in date, signature of customer

4.3   **(a)**   Invoice 392 is for £690 and not for £590

   (b)   Credit note 295 for £90 has not been allowed for on the remittance advice

5 Chapter activities – answers
Process documents from suppliers

5.1   delivery note

5.2   the purchases ledger

5.3   purchases

5.4

(a)   Who has supplied the chairs?

Helicon Furniture

(b)   What is the problem with the consignment?

2 chairs damaged

(c)   What document would be issued by the supplier to adjust the account of Praxis Stationery?

credit note

(d)   Where in the supplier's accounting records would the account of Praxis Stationery be maintained?

sales ledger

5.5 Has the correct purchase price of the chairs been charged? Yes or No?   YES

Has the correct discount been applied? Yes or No?   NO

What would be the VAT amount charged if the invoice was correct?   £252.00

What would be the total amount charged if the invoice was correct?   £1,692.00

5.6 Has the correct number of tables been supplied? Yes or No?   NO

Has the correct type of table been supplied? Yes or No?   NO

What will be the total of the invoice on the basis of the details on the delivery note?   £376.00

If a credit note were issued, what would be the total, including VAT?   £75.20

Chapter activities – answers

6 Accounting for purchases and purchases returns

6.1 purchases invoice

6.2 invoice received; purchases day book; purchases account; purchases ledger control account; supplier's account

6.3 debit purchases; debit VAT; credit purchases ledger control

6.4 (a)

Purchases Day Book						PDB55
Date	Details	Invoice number	Reference	Total	VAT	Net
20-2				£	£	£
3 May	Malvern Manufacturing	7321	PL625	199.75	29.75	170.00
9 May	S Burston	SB745	PL530	311.37	46.37	265.00
12 May	Iley Supplies Ltd	4721	PL605	528.75	78.75	450.00
18 May	SG Enterprises	3947	PL720	969.37	144.37	825.00
23 May	S Burston	SB773	PL530	501.72	74.72	427.00
30 May	Malvern Manufacturing	7408	PL625	427.70	63.70	364.00
31 May	Totals for month			2,938.66	437.66	2,501.00
				GL2350	GL2200	GL5100

(b) **GENERAL LEDGER**

Dr		Value Added Tax Account (GL2200)			Cr
20-2			£	20-2	£
31 May	Purchases Day Book	PDB55	437.66		

Dr		Purchases Ledger Control Account (GL2350)			Cr
20-2			£	20-2	£
				31 May Purchases Day Book PDB55	2,938.66

Dr				**Purchases Account** (GL5100)			Cr
20-2			£	20-2			£
31 May	Purchases Day Book	PDB55	2,501.00				

PURCHASES LEDGER

Dr				**S Burston** (PL530)			Cr
20-2			£	20-2			£
				9 May	Purchases	PDB55	311.37
				23 May	Purchases	PDB55	501.72

Dr				**Iley Supplies Limited** (PL605)			Cr
20-2			£	20-2			£
				12 May	Purchases	PDB55	528.75

Dr				**Malvern Manufacturing** (PL625)			Cr
20-2			£	20-2			£
				3 May	Purchases	PDB55	199.75
				30 May	Purchases	PDB55	427.70

Dr				**SG Enterprises** (PL720)			Cr
20-2			£	20-2			£
				18 May	Purchases	PDB55	969.37

6.5 (a)

Purchases Returns Day Book					PRDB14

Date	Details	Credit note number	Reference	Total	VAT	Net
20-2				£	£	£
11 May	Malvern Manufacturing	CN345	PL625	82.25	12.25	70.00
17 May	Iley Supplies Ltd	CN241	PL605	99.87	14.87	85.00
24 May	SG Enterprises	85	PL720	29.37	4.37	25.00
31 May	S Burston	SB95	PL530	64.62	9.62	55.00
31 May	Totals for month			276.11	41.11	235.00
				GL2350	GL2200	GL5110

(b)   **GENERAL LEDGER**

Dr   **Value Added Tax Account** (GL2200)   Cr

20-2		£	20-2		£
31 May Purchases Day Book	PDB55	437.66	31 May Purchases Returns Day Book	PRDB14	41.11

Dr   **Purchases Ledger Control Account** (GL2350)   Cr

20-2		£	20-2		£
31 May Purchases Returns Day Book	PRDB14	276.11	31 May Purchases Day Book	PDB55	2,938.66

Dr   **Purchases Returns Account** (GL5110)   Cr

20-2		£	20-2		£
			31 May Purchases Returns Day Book	PRDB14	235.00

PURCHASES LEDGER

Dr   **S Burston** (PL530)   Cr

20-2		£	20-2		£
31 May Purchases Returns	PRDB14	64.62	9 May Purchases	PDB55	311.37
			23 May Purchases	PDB55	501.72

Dr			**Iley Supplies Limited** (PL605)			Cr
20-2		£	20-2			£
17 May Purchases Returns			12 May Purchases	PDB55	528.75
	PRDB14	99.87				

Dr			**Malvern Manufacturing** (PL625)			Cr
20-2		£	20-2			£
11 May Purchases Returns			3 May Purchases	PDB55	199.75
	PRDB14	82.25	30 May Purchases	PDB55	427.70

Dr			**SG Enterprises** (PL720)			Cr
20-2		£	20-2			£
24 May Purchases Returns			18 May Purchases	PDB55	969.37
	PRDB14	29.37				

6.6   Purchases day book

Date 20XX	Details	Invoice number	Total £	VAT £	Net £	Purchases type 1 £	Purchases type 2 £
30 June	King & Co	K641	1,974	294	1,680		1,680
30 June	Rossingtons	2129	3,008	448	2,560	2,560	
30 June	Moniz Ltd	M/149	2,162	322	1,840		1,840
	Totals		7,144	1,064	6,080	2,560	3,520

6.7 (a)

Purchases ledger

Account name	Amount £	Debit ✓	Credit ✓
H & L Ltd	6,392		✓
Sperrin & Co	2,162		✓
Hickmores	4,512		✓
Marklew plc	1,081		✓

General ledger

Account name	Amount £	Debit ✓	Credit ✓
Purchases	12,040	✓	
Value Added Tax	2,107	✓	
Purchases ledger control	14,147		✓

(b)

Purchases ledger

Account name	Amount £	Debit ✓	Credit ✓
Marcer Transport	611	✓	
Schuller Ltd	423	✓	

General ledger

Account name	Amount £	Debit ✓	Credit ✓
Purchases returns	880		✓
Value Added Tax	154		✓
Purchases ledger control	1,034	✓	

7 Chapter activities – answers
Prepare payments to suppliers

7.1   an increase in the total amount owing shown on the statement of account

7.2   purchase invoices, purchase credit notes, total amount owing

7.3   will reduce the total amount shown as owing on the statement of account

7.4   **(a)**   Cheque for £1,000

   (b)   invoice 790

   (c)   £360

7.5   **(a)**   the BACS remittance advice will be sent without a cheque to A Strauss & Co

   (b)   30 April

   (c)   Invoice 2461, invoice 2479, credit note CN105

   (d)   £3,640

8	**Chapter activities – answers** **Cash book**

8.1   debit purchases £200; debit VAT £35; credit bank £235

8.2   the debit side of discount allowed account

8.3   the debit side of VAT account

8.4   (a)   **Sales ledger**

Account name	Amount £	Debit ✓	Credit ✓
Smithsons Ltd	2,750		✓
Smithsons Ltd	100		✓

(b)   **General ledger**

Account name	Amount £	Debit ✓	Credit ✓
Discounts allowed	100	✓	
Sales ledger control	2,750		✓
Sales ledger control	100		✓
Wages	1,175	✓	
Rent	1,200	✓	
Stationery	600	✓	
Value Added Tax	105	✓	

8.5 (a) True

(b) False – the balance b/d of £402 on 1 October shows that, according to the cash book, there is a bank overdraft.

(c) **GENERAL LEDGER**

Dr		**Sales Account**			Cr
20-1		£	20-1		£
			30 Sep Bank	CB68	440

Dr		**Sales Ledger Control Account**			Cr
20-1		£	20-1		£
			30 Sep Bank	CB68	1,580
			30 Sep Discount allowed	CB68	25

Dr		**Purchases Ledger Control Account**			Cr
20-1		£	20-1		£
30 Sep Bank	CB68	1,940			
30 Sep Discount received	CB68	30			

Dr		**Purchases Account**			Cr
20-1		£	20-1		£
30 Sep Bank	CB68	160			

Dr		**General Expenses Account**			Cr
20-1		£	20-1		£
30 Sep Bank	CB68	640			

Dr		**Wages Account**			Cr
20-1		£	20-1		£
30 Sep Bank	CB68	1,254			

Dr		**Office Equipment Account**			Cr
20-1		£	20-1		£
30 Sep Bank	CB68	1,200			

Dr		**Discount Allowed Account**			Cr
20-1		£	20-1		£
30 Sep Bank	CB68	25			

Dr			**Discount Received Account**			Cr
20-1			£	20-1		£
				30 Sep	Bank	CB68	30

Dr			**Value Added Tax Account**			Cr
20-1			£	20-1		£
30 Sep	Bank	CB68	350	30 Sep	Bank	CB68	77

(d)

SALES LEDGER

Dr			**Albany Limited**			Cr
20-1			£	20-1		£
				30 Sep	Bank	CB68	1,580
				30 Sep	Discount allowed	CB68	25

PURCHASES LEDGER

Dr			**Nelson Stores**			Cr
20-1			£	20-1		£
30 Sep	Bank	CB68	1,940			
30 Sep	Discount received	CB68	30			

8.6   (a)   **Sales ledger**

Account name	Amount £	Debit ✓	Credit ✓
Boscawen Ltd	1,540		✓
Boscawen Ltd	45		✓

(b)   **General ledger**

Account name	Amount £	Debit ✓	Credit ✓
Discounts allowed	45	✓	
Sales ledger control	1,540		✓
Sales ledger control	45		✓

(c)   **General ledger**

Account name	Amount £	Debit ✓	Credit ✓
Wages	1,265	✓	
Office equipment	1,640	✓	
Value Added Tax	287	✓	

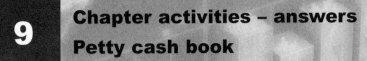

9

Chapter activities – answers
Petty cash book

9.1   the petty cash float is restored to the same amount for the beginning of each week or month

9.2   debit petty cash control £108; credit bank £108

9.3

Statement	True ✓	False ✓
payments made from petty cash book are recorded on the debit side		✓
a petty cash book may combine the roles of a book of prime entry and double-entry book-keeping	✓	
petty cash vouchers are authorised for payments by the petty cashier		✓
the totals of the petty cash analysis columns are transferred to general ledger where they are debited to the appropriate expense account	✓	

9.4 General ledger

Account name	Amount £	Debit ✓	Credit ✓
Petty cash book	110	✓	
Bank	110		✓

9.5 General ledger

Account name	Amount £	Debit ✓	Credit ✓
VAT	4.90	✓	
Postage	11.50	✓	
Travel expenses	34.75	✓	
Stationery	15.60	✓	
Bank	57.00		✓

9.6 (a)

GENERAL LEDGER

Dr				Value Added Tax Account			Cr
20-6			£	20-6			£
31 Jul	Petty cash book	PCB35	3.78				

Dr				Travel Account			Cr
20-6			£	20-6			£
31 Jul	Petty cash book	PCB35	26.00				

Dr				Postages Account			Cr
20-6			£	20-6			£
31 Jul	Petty cash book	PCB35	11.55	14 Jul	Petty cash book	PCB35	6.25

Dr				Stationery Account			Cr
20-6			£	20-6			£
31 Jul	Petty cash book	PCB35	13.20				

Dr				Meals Account			Cr
20-6			£	20-6			£
31 Jul	Petty cash book	PCB35	10.00				

Dr				Purchases Ledger Control Account			Cr
20-6			£	20-6			£
31 Jul	Petty cash book	PCB35	18.25				

Dr				Petty Cash Control Account			Cr
20-6			£	20-6			£
1 Jul	Balance b/d		200.00	31 Jul	Petty cash book	PCB35	82.78
31 Jul	Petty cash book	PCB35	6.25	31 Jul	Balance c/d		200.00
31 Jul	Bank	CB	76.53				
			282.78				282.78
1 Aug	Balance b/d		200.00				

Dr		Cash Book				Cr
20-6		Bank	20-6			Bank
			31 Jul	Petty cash	PCB35	76.53

(b)

PURCHASES LEDGER

Dr				J Clarke			Cr
20-6			£	20-6			£
31 Jul	Petty cash book	PCB35	18.25				

10 Chapter activities – answers
Balancing accounts, the accounting equation, capital and revenue

10.1 (a), (b) & (c)

Vehicle expenses

Date 20XX	Details	Amount £	Date 20XX	Details	Amount £
01 Jun	Balance b/f	2,055	30 Jun	Balance c/d	2,275
23 Jun	Bank	220			
	Total	2,275		Total	2,275
01 Jul	Balance b/d	2,275			

Discounts received

Date 20XX	Details	Amount £	Date 20XX	Details	Amount £
30 Jun	Balance c/d	840	01 Jun	Balance b/f	725
			30 Jun	Purchases ledger control	115
	Total	840		Total	840
			01 Jul	Balance b/d	840

Commission received

Date 20XX	Details	Amount £	Date 20XX	Details	Amount £
30 Jun	Balance c/d	3,145	01 Jun	Balance b/f	2,680
			19 Jun	Bank	465
	Total	3,145		Total	3,145
			01 Jul	Balance b/d	3,145

10.2   (a)

Statement	True ✓	False ✓
Liabilities equals capital plus assets		✓
Assets equals liabilities minus capital		✓
Capital equals assets minus liabilities	✓	

(b)

Item	Asset ✓	Liability ✓
Vehicles	✓	
Bank loan		✓
Money owing by receivables (debtors)	✓	
Inventory (stock)	✓	
Cash	✓	
VAT owing to HM Revenue and Customs		✓

10.3

Assets	Liabilities	Capital
£	£	£
50,000	0	50,000
40,000	10,000	30,000
55,200	24,950	30,250
58,980	18,220	40,760
40,320	15,980	24,340
73,350	24,760	48,590

10.4   (a) - (b)   Vehicles have been bought for £10,000, paid from the bank

(b) - (c)   Inventory (stock) has been bought for £6,000, paid from the bank

(c) - (d)   Inventory (stock) has been bought £3,000, on credit from a supplier

(d) - (e)   Further vehicle bought for £8,000, paid for with £3,000 from the bank and a loan for £5,000

(e) - (f)   Owner introduces £10,000 additional capital, paid into the bank

10.5

Item	Capital expenditure ✓	Revenue expenditure ✓	Capital income ✓	Revenue income ✓
Purchase of vehicles	✓			
Fuel for vehicles		✓		
Discounts received				✓
Receipts from sale of office equipment			✓	
Redecoration of property		✓		
Extension to property	✓			
Receipts from sale of goods to credit customers				✓
Delivery cost of new machine	✓			
Increase in owner's capital			✓	
Repairs to vehicles		✓		

11 Chapter activities – answers
The initial trial balance

11.1 sales account

11.2 sales ledger control account

11.3 **Trial balance of Kate Trelawney as at 31 March 20-2**

Name of account	Dr £	Cr £
Bank loan		3,650
Purchases	23,745	
Vehicle	9,500	
Sales		65,034
Bank	2,162	
Discount allowed	317	
Purchases returns		855
Sales ledger control	7,045	
Office equipment	5,450	
Inventory (stock) at 1 April 20-1	4,381	
Sales returns	1,624	
Purchases ledger control		4,736
Expenses	32,598	
Discount received		494
Capital *(missing figure)*		12,053
	86,822	86,822

11.4

Account name	Amount £	Debit £	Credit £
Bank overdraft	4,293		4,293
Loan from bank	12,500		12,500
Vehicles	25,500	25,500	
Inventory (stock)	10,417	10,417	
Petty cash control	68	68	
Capital	25,794		25,794
VAT owing to HM Revenue and Customs	1,496		1,496
Purchases ledger control	12,794		12,794
Purchases	104,763	104,763	
Purchases returns	2,681		2,681
Sales ledger control	28,354	28,354	
Sales	184,267		184,267
Sales returns	4,098	4,098	
Discount allowed	1,312	1,312	
Discount received	1,784		1,784
Wages	35,961	35,961	
Telephone	3,474	3,474	
Advertising	5,921	5,921	
Insurance	3,084	3,084	
Heating and lighting	2,477	2,477	
Rent and rates	3,672	3,672	
Postages	876	876	
Miscellaneous expenses	545	545	
Drawings	15,087	15,087	
Totals	–	245,609	245,609

11.5

Account name	Amount £	Debit £	Credit £
Sales	262,394		262,394
Sales returns	2,107	2,107	
Sales ledger control	33,844	33,844	
Purchases	157,988	157,988	
Purchases returns	1,745		1,745
Purchases ledger control	17,311		17,311
Discount received	1,297		1,297
Discount allowed	845	845	
Rent and rates	5,941	5,941	
Advertising	6,088	6,088	
Insurance	3,176	3,176	
Wages	48,954	48,954	
Heating and lighting	4,266	4,266	
Postages and telephone	2,107	2,107	
Miscellaneous expenses	632	632	
Vehicles	28,400	28,400	
Capital	48,756		48,756
Drawings	19,354	19,354	
Office equipment	10,500	10,500	
Inventory (stock)	16,246	16,246	
Petty cash control	150	150	
Bank (debit balance)	3,096	3,096	
VAT owing to HM Revenue and Customs	3,721		3,721
Loan from bank	8,470		8,470
Totals	–	343,694	343,694

Basic accounting 1

Practice assessment 1

Time allowance: 2 hours

- This Assessment relates to the accounting system of Sidbury Traders.
- The accounting system of Sidbury Traders keeps the cash book and petty cash book as books of prime entry and as double-entry accounts in the general ledger.
- Each task of the Assessment is to be answered separately.
- The rate of Value Added Tax used is 17.5%.

Section 1

Task 1.1

The following credit transactions all took place on 30 June and have been entered into the sales day book as shown below. No entries have yet been made in the ledgers.

Sales day book

Date 20XX	Details	Invoice number	Total £	VAT £	Net £
30 Jun	Durning Ltd	1520	1,081	161	920
30 Jun	Perran & Co	1521	4,089	609	3,480
30 Jun	Beacon Traders	1522	5,922	882	5,040
30 Jun	Zelah plc	1523	2,209	329	1,880
	Totals		13,301	1,981	11,320

(a) **What will be the entries in the sales ledger?**

Select your account name from the following list: Beacon Traders, Durning Ltd, Perran & Co, Purchases, Purchases ledger control, Purchases returns, Sales, Sales ledger control, Sales returns, Value Added Tax, Zelah plc.

Sales ledger

Account name	Amount £	Debit ✓	Credit ✓

(b)   **What will be the entries in the general ledger?**

Select your account name from the following list: Purchases, Purchases ledger control, Purchases returns, Sales, Sales ledger control, Sales returns.

General ledger

Account name	Amount £	Debit ✓	Credit ✓

Task 1.2

The following credit transactions all took place on 30 June and have been entered into the purchases returns day book as shown below. No entries have yet been made in the ledgers.

Purchases returns day book

Date 20XX	Details	Credit note number	Total £	VAT £	Net £
30 Jun	Mithian & Co	1684	799	119	680
30 Jun	Bolster Stores	C414	517	77	440
	Totals		1,316	196	1,120

(a)   **What will be the entries in the purchases ledger?**

Select your account name from the following list: Bolster Stores, Mithian & Co, Purchases, Purchases ledger control, Purchases returns, Sales, Sales ledger control, Sales returns, Value Added Tax.

Purchases ledger

Account name	Amount £	Debit ✓	Credit ✓

(b) **What will be the entries in the general ledger?**

Select your account name from the following list: Bolster Stores, Mithian & Co, Purchases, Purchases ledger control, Purchases returns, Sales, Sales ledger control, Sales returns, Value Added Tax.

General ledger

Account name	Amount £	Debit ✓	Credit ✓

Task 1.3

The following transactions all took place on 30 June and have been entered in the debit side of the cash book as shown below. No entries have yet been made in the ledgers.

Cash book – Debit side

Date 20XX	Details	Discounts £	Bank £
30 Jun	Balance b/f		1,352
30 Jun	Crossways Ltd	100	4,000

(a) **What will be the entries in the sales ledger?**

Select your account name from the following list: Balance b/f, Bank, Crossways Ltd, Discounts allowed, Discounts received, Purchases ledger control, Sales ledger control.

Sales ledger

Account name	Amount £	Debit ✓	Credit ✓

(b)   What will be the entries in the general ledger?

Select your account name from the following list: Balance b/f, Bank, Crossways Ltd, Discounts allowed, Discounts received, Purchases ledger control, Sales ledger control.

General ledger

Account name	Amount £	Debit ✓	Credit ✓

The following transactions all took place on 30 June and have been entered in the credit side of the cash book as shown below. No entries have yet been made in the ledgers.

Cash book – Credit side

Date 20XX	Details	VAT £	Bank £
30 Jun	Stationery	21	141
30 Jun	Rent		200

(c)   What will be the entries in the general ledger?

Select your account name from the following list: Bank, Purchases ledger control, Rent, Sales ledger control, Stationery, Value Added Tax.

General ledger

Account name	Amount £	Debit ✓	Credit ✓

Task 1.4

Sidbury Traders maintains a petty cash book as both a book of prime entry and part of the double-entry accounting system. The following transactions all took place on 30 June and have been entered in the petty cash book as shown below. No entries have yet been made in the general ledger.

Petty cash book

Date	Details	Amount	Date	Details	Amount	VAT	Postage	Travel expenses	Office expenses
20XX		£	20XX		£	£	£	£	£
30 Jun	Balance b/f	94.00	30 Jun	Stationery	23.97	3.57			20.40
30 Jun	Bank	56.00	30 Jun	Post office	12.00		12.00		
			30 Jun	Rail fare	20.50			20.50	
			30 Jun	Printer supplies	25.85	3.85			22.00
				Balance c/d	67.68				
		150.00			150.00	7.42	12.00	20.50	42.40

What will be the entries in the general ledger?

Select your account name from the following list: Balance b/f, Balance c/d, Bank, Office expenses, Petty cash book, Postage, Post office, Printer supplies, Rail fare, Stationery, Travel expenses, Value Added Tax.

General ledger

Account name	Amount £	Debit ✓	Credit ✓

Task 1.5

The following two accounts are in the general ledger at the close of the day on 30 June.

(a)   **Insert the balance carried down together with date and details**

(b)   **Insert the totals**

(c)   **Insert the balance brought down together with date and details**

Select your account name from the following list: Balance b/f, Balance c/d, Bank, Closing balance, Opening balance, Sales ledger control

Discounts allowed

Date 20XX	Details	Amount £	Date 20XX	Details	Amount £
01 Jun	Balance b/f	640			
26 Jun	Sales ledger control	145			
	Total			Total	

Select your account name from the following list: Balance b/f, Balance c/d, Bank, Closing balance, Opening balance, Sales ledger control

Rent received

Date 20XX	Details	Amount £	Date 20XX	Details	Amount £
			01 Jun	Balance b/f	2,350
			22 Jun	Bank	450
	Total			Total	

Task 1.6

Below is a list of balances to be transferred to the trial balance as at 30 June.

Place the figures in the debit or credit column, as appropriate, and total each column.

Account name	Amount £	Debit £	Credit £
Vehicles	15,390		
Bank overdraft	1,270		
Petty cash control	112		
Inventory (stock)	9,345		
Capital	31,796		
Drawings	6,290		
VAT owing to HM Revenue and Customs	2,317		
Loan from bank	5,650		
Purchases	22,685		
Sales ledger control	8,351		
Purchases returns	1,248		
Sales	46,854		
Purchases ledger control	6,382		
Sales returns	1,685		
Discount received	817		
Discount allowed	621		
Administration	18,341		
Advertising	4,057		
Hotel expenses	1,298		
Heating and lighting	1,836		
Rent and rates	3,494		
Travel costs	1,022		
Telephone	874		
Miscellaneous expenses	933		
Totals	–		

Section 2

Task 2.1

Sales invoices have been prepared and partially entered in the **sales day book**, as shown below.

(a)   **Complete the entries in the sales day book by inserting the appropriate figures for each invoice**

(b)   **Total the last five columns of the sales day book**

Sales day book

Date 20XX	Details	Invoice number	Total £	VAT £	Net £	Sales type 1 £	Sales type 2 £
30 Jun	T Singh	4751	4,230	630	3,600		3,600
30 Jun	RMG Ltd	4752	1,645	245	1,400	1,400	
30 Jun	Wills Ltd	4753	329	49	280	280	
	Totals		6,204	924	5,280	1,680	3,600

Task 2.2

A supply of batteries has been delivered to Sidbury Traders by Electrical Supplies. The purchase order sent from Sidbury Traders, and the invoice from Electrical Supplies, are shown below.

Sidbury Traders

29 Constitution Street

Mereford, MR11 4GT

Purchase Order No. ST1872

To: Electrical Supplies

Date: 9 July 20XX

Please supply 200 packs of AA batteries product code 6543AA

Purchase price: £5 per pack, plus VAT

Discount: less 25% trade discount, as agreed.

INVOICE   Electrical Supplies

Unit 16 Varsity Estate, Spirefield SP6 3DF

VAT Registration No. 118 3822 39

Invoice No. 2363
Sidbury Traders
29 Constitution Street
Mereford, MR11 4GT

12 July 20XX

200	Packs AA batteries @ £5.00 per pack less trade discount	£800.00
	VAT @ 17.5%	£140.00
	Total	£940.00

Terms: 30 days net

Check the invoice against the purchase order and answer the following questions.

Has the correct purchase price of the batteries been charged? Yes or No?

Has the correct discount been applied? Yes or No?

What would be the VAT amount charged if the invoice was correct?

What would be the total amount charged if the invoice was correct?

Task 2.3

Sidbury Traders codes all purchase invoices with a supplier code and a general ledger code. A selection of the codes used is given below.

Supplier	Supplier Account Code
Delta Ltd	DEL08
Electrical Supplies	ELE10
Elemox & Co	ELE14
Expo Products	EXP04
Faraday Ltd	FAR02

Item	General Ledger Code
Electrical goods	GL380
Tools	GL385
Timber	GL390
Paints	GL395
Plumbing	GL400

This is an invoice received from a supplier.

INVOICE   **Electrical Supplies**

Unit 16 Varsity Estate, Spirefield SP6 3DF

VAT Registration No. 118 3822 39

Invoice No. 2370
Sidbury Traders
29 Constitution Street
Mereford, MR11 4GT

22 July 20XX

50	Screwdriver sets @ £2.40 each less trade discount	£90.00
	VAT @ 17.5%	£ 15.75
	Total	£105.75

Select which codes would be used to code this invoice.

(a)   Select your supplier account code from the following list:

DEL08, ELE10, ELE14, EXP04, FAR02, GL380, GL385, GL390, GL395, GL400

```
```

(b)   Select your general ledger account code from the following list:

DEL08, ELE10, ELE14, EXP04, FAR02, GL380, GL385, GL390, GL395, GL400

```
```

(c)   State which two codes would be used if the supply had been made by Expo Products and had been a consignment of gloss paint.

```
```

Task 2.4

Shown below is a statement of account received from G French & Co, a credit supplier, and the supplier's account as shown in the purchases ledger of Sidbury Traders.

G French & Co
17 Highfield Grove, West Mereford, MR2 7GH

To: Sidbury Traders

29 Constitution Street

Mereford, MR11 4GT   **STATEMENT OF ACCOUNT**

Date 20XX	Invoice Number	Details	Invoice Amount £	Cheque Amount £	Balance £
1 June	1685	Goods	8,000		8,000
2 June	1687	Goods	2,600		10,600
8 June	1696	Goods	700		11,300
26 June	1752	Goods	1,500		12,800
1 July	-	Cheque		8,000	4,800

			G French & Co			
Date 20XX	Details		Amount £	Date 20XX	Details	Amount £
1 July	Bank		8,000	1 June	Purchases	8,000
25 July	Bank		4,000	7 June	Purchases	2,600
				10 June	Purchases	700

(a)   Which item is missing from the statement of account from G French & Co? *Select your answer from the following list:*

Invoice 1685, Invoice 1687, Invoice 1696, Invoice 1752, Cheque for £8,000, Cheque for £4,000

(b)   Which item is missing from the supplier account in Sidbury Traders' purchases ledger? *Select your answer from the following list:*

Invoice 1685, Invoice 1687, Invoice 1696, Invoice 1752, Cheque for £8,000, Cheque for £4,000

(c)   Assuming any differences between the statement of account from G French & Co and the supplier account in Sidbury Traders' purchases ledger are simply due to omission errors, what is the amount owing to G French & Co?

£

Task 2.5

Sidbury Traders sends BACS remittance advice notes to suppliers on the last day of the month following the month of invoice. Sidbury Traders banks with National Bank plc and Amici Ltd banks with Western Bank plc. Below is an uncompleted BACS remittance advice and an extract from Sidbury Trader's purchases ledger.

Sidbury Traders

29 Constitution Street

Mereford, MR11 4GT

BACS REMITTANCE ADVICE

To: Date:

The following payment will reach your bank account within 3 working days.

Invoice number	Credit note number	Amount £
	Total amount paid	

Amici Ltd					
Date	*Details*	*Amount*	*Date*	*Details*	*Amount*
20XX		£	*20XX*		£
16 Feb	Purchases returns credit note CN204	400	15 Feb	Purchases Invoice 1250	1,750
19 Feb	Purchases returns credit note CN232	270	20 Mar	Purchases Invoice 1263	3,650
30 Mar	Bank	1,080	29 Mar	Purchases Invoice 1301	1,105
			10 Apl	Purchases Invoice 1350	720

(a)   To whom will the BACS remittance advice be addressed? (Select one)

Sidbury Traders   National Bank plc   Western Bank plc

(b)   What will be the date shown on the BACS remittance advice? (Select one)

1 May   28 Feb   31 Mar

(c)   What will be the TWO items shown on the BACS remittance advice?

	✔
Purchase invoice number 1250	
Purchase invoice number 1263	
Purchase invoice number 1301	
Purchase invoice number 1350	
Purchase credit note number 204	
Purchase credit note number 232	

(d)   What will be the total amount paid?

£

(e)   Which of the following statements is true? (Select one)   ✔

The BACS remittance advice informs Central Bank of the amount payable to Sidbury Traders	
The BACS remittance advice informs the supplier of the amount payable into its account at Western Bank	
The BACS remittance advice informs the supplier of the amount payable by Amici Ltd Ltd	
The BACS remittance advice informs the National Bank of how much will be paid into the account of Sidbury Traders	

Task 2.6

On 1 July Sidbury Traders delivered the following goods to a credit customer, Bow Street DIY.

Sidbury Traders

29 Constitution Street

Mereford, MR11 4GT

Delivery note No. 21765

Date: 9 July 20XX

Bow Street DIY
20 Penarth Road
Bow Street
Ceredigion, SY56 2AW

Customer account code: BS152

---

10 Supathrust Power Drill product code PD124.

The list price of the drills was £56 each plus VAT at 17.5%. Bow Street DIY are to be given a 20% trade discount and a 5% early settlement discount.

(a) Complete the invoice below

Sidbury Traders

29 Constitution Street

Mereford, MR11 4GT

VAT Registration No. 298 3827 04

Bow Street DIY
20 Penarth Road
Bow Street
Ceredigion, SY56 2AW

Invoice No: 1298

Customer account code:

Delivery note number:

Date: 9 July 20XX

Quantity	Code	Unit price £	Total £	Net amount £	VAT(17.5%) £	Gross £

(b) What would be the amount payable on this invoice if the settlement (cash) discount was taken by Bow Street DIY?

Select your answer from the following options:

	✔
£448.00	
£500.08	
£522.48	
£658.00	

Task 2.7

The following is a summary of transactions with Broadsword Trading, a new credit customer.

£450 re invoice 1301 of 10 August

£1,210 re invoice 1370 of 12 August

£45 re credit note 346 of 21 August

£720 re invoice 1412 of 27 August

Cheque for £405 received 30 August

Complete the statement of account below.

Sidbury Traders

29 Constitution Street
Mereford, MR11 4GT

To: Broadsword Trading   Date: 31 August 20XX

Date 20XX	Details	Transaction amount £	Outstanding amount £
10 August	Invoice 1301		
12 August	Invoice 1370		
21 August	Credit note 346		
27 August	Invoice 1412		
30 August	Cheque		

Task 2.8

The account shown below is in the sales ledger of Sidbury Traders. A cheque for £1,300 was received from this customer on 2 July.

M Khan					
Date 20XX	Details	Amount £	Date 20XX	Details	Amount £
1 June	Balance b/f	4,620	2 June	Bank	4,620
22 June	Sales invoice 1201	1,962	26 June	Sales returns credit note 295	662
30 June	Sales Invoice 1262	2,850			

(a) Which item has not been included in the payment?

Select your account name from the following list:

Balance b/f, Sales invoice 1201, Sales invoice 1262, Bank, Sales returns credit note 295

(b) A further sales invoice was issued to M Khan for £2,340 on 2 July. What was the amount outstanding on the account on 3 July? No further payments had been received or other transactions made since 30 June.

£

(c) Sidbury Traders on 1 July offered M Khan an extra discount of 5% on invoices of value of £3,000 or more. This is known as:

	✔
Settlement discount	
Trade discount	
Bulk discount	

Task 2.9

It is important to understand the difference between capital expenditure, revenue expenditure, capital income and revenue income.

Select one option in each instance below to show whether the item will be capital expenditure, revenue expenditure, capital income or revenue income.

Item	Capital expenditure ✓	Revenue expenditure ✓	Capital income ✓	Revenue income ✓
Payments for purchases of goods from credit suppliers				
Purchase of office equipment				
Rent received				
Receipt from sale of vehicle				
Receipts from sales				
Bank loan received				

Task 2.10

Financial accounting is based upon the accounting equation.

(a)   **Show whether the following statements are true or false.**

Statement	True ✓	False ✓
Assets equals capital plus liabilities		
Capital equals assets plus liabilities		
Assets minus liabilities equals capital		

(b)   **Classify each of the following items as an asset or a liability.**

Item	Asset ✓	Liability ✓
Bank overdraft		
Office equipment		
Money owing to payables (creditors)		

Basic accounting 1

Practice assessment 2

Time allowance: 2 hours

- This Assessment is based on a sample assessment provided by the AAT and is reproduced here with their kind permission.

- This Assessment relates to the accounting system of Kitchen Kuts.

- The accounting system of Kitchen Kuts keeps the cash book and petty cash book as books of prime entry and as double-entry accounts in the general ledger.

- Each task of the Assessment is to be answered separately.

- The rate of Value Added Tax used is 17.5%.

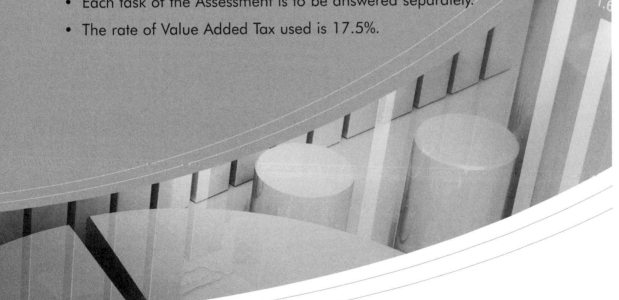

SECTION 1

Task 1.1

The following transactions all took place on 30 June and have been entered into the sales day book as shown below. No entries have yet been made into the ledger system.

Date 20XX	Details	Invoice number	Total £	VAT @ 17.5% £	Net
30 Jun	West and Webb	1600	9,400	1,400	8,000
30 Jun	Kelly and Co	1601	11,280	1,680	9,600
30 Jun	Bradley Delights	1602	3,854	574	3,280
30 Jun	Burgess Wholesale	1603	7,191	1,071	6,120
Totals			31,725	4,725	27,000

(a) What will be the entries in the subsidiary (sales) ledger?

Select your account name from the following list:

Bradley Delights, Burgess Wholesale, Kelly and Co, Purchases, Purchases ledger control, Purchases returns, Sales, Sales ledger control, Sales returns, VAT, West and Webb

Account name	Amount £	Debit ✓	Credit ✓

(b) What will be the entries in the main ledger?

Select your account name from the following list:

Purchases ledger control, Sales, Sales ledger control, Sales returns, VAT

Account name	Amount £	Debit ✓	Credit ✓

Task 1.2

The following credit transactions all took place on 30 June and have been entered into the purchases returns day-book as shown below. No entries have yet been made in the ledgers.

Purchases returns day-book

Date 20XX	Details	Credit note number	Total £	VAT £	Net £
30 June	Hanover Ltd	1499	2,115	315	1,800
30 June	Lawson Ltd	PO1098	470	70	400
Totals			2,585	385	2,200

(a) What will be the entries in the purchases ledger?

Purchases ledger

Account name	Amount £	Debit ✓	Credit ✓

Select your account name from the following list:

Hanover Ltd, Lawson Ltd, Net, Purchases, Purchases ledger control, Purchases returns, Sales, Sales ledger control, Sales returns, Total, VAT

(b) What will be the entries in the general ledger?

General ledger

Account name	Amount £	Debit ✓	Credit ✓

Select your account name from the following list:

Hanover Ltd, Lawson Ltd, Net, Purchases, Purchases ledger control, Purchases returns, Sales, Sales ledger control, Sales returns, Total, VAT

Task 1.3

The following transactions all took place on 30 June and have been entered in the debit side of the cash-book as shown below. No entries have yet been made in the ledgers.

Cash-book – Debit side

Date 20XX	Details		Discounts £	Bank £
30 Jun	Balance b/f			5,236
30 Jun	RBL Ltd		150	6,000

(a) What will be the TWO entries in the sales ledger?

Sales ledger

Account name	Amount £	Debit ✓	Credit ✓

Select your account name from the following list:

Balance b/f, Bank, Discounts allowed, Discounts received, Purchases ledger control, RBL Ltd, Sales ledger control

(b) What will be the THREE entries in the general ledger?

General ledger

Account name	Amount £	Debit ✓	Credit ✓

Select your account name from the following list:

Balance b/f, Bank, Discounts allowed, Discounts received, Purchases ledger control, RBL Ltd, Sales ledger control

The following transactions all took place on 30 June and have been entered in the credit side of the cash-book as shown below. No entries have yet been made in the ledgers.

Cash-book – Credit side

Date 20XX	Details		VAT £	Bank £
30 Jun	Office expenses		14	94
30 Jun	Insurance			400

(c)   What will be the entries in the general ledger?

General ledger

Account name	Amount £	Debit ✓	Credit ✓

Select your account name from the following list:

Bank, Insurance, Office expenses, Purchases ledger control, Sales ledger control, VAT

Task 1.4

Kitchen Kuts maintains a petty cash book as both a book of prime entry and part of the double entry accounting system. The following transactions all took place on 30 June and have been entered in the petty cash-book as shown below. No entries have yet been made in the general ledger.

Petty cash-book

Date 20XX	Details	Amount	Date 20XX	Details	Amount	VAT	Postage	Motor expenses	Office expenses
		£			£	£	£		£
30 Jun	Balance b/f	118.00	30 Jun	Fuel	18.80	2.80		16.00	
30 Jun	Bank	82.00	30 Jun	Post office	20.00		20.00		
			30 Jun	Motor repair	42.30	6.30		36.00	
			30 Jun	Envelopes	14.10	2.10			12.00
			30 Jun	Balance c/d	104.80				
		200.00			200.00	11.20	20.00	52.00	12.00

What will be the FIVE entries in the general ledger?

General ledger

Account name	Amount £	Debit ✓	Credit ✓

Select your account name from the following list:

Balance b/f, Balance c/d, Bank, Envelopes, Fuel, Motor expenses, Motor repair, Office expenses, Petty cash-book, Post Office, Postage, VAT

Task 1.5

The following two accounts are in the main ledger at the close of day on 30 June.

(a) Insert the balance carried down together with date and details.

(b) Insert the totals.

(c) Insert the balance brought down together with date and details.

Telephone

Date 20XX	Details	Amount £	Date 20XX	Details	Amount £
01 Jun	Balance b/f	1,320			
26 Jun	Bank	279			
	Total				

Select your account name from the following list:

Balance b/d, Balance c/d, Bank, Closing balance, Opening balance, Purchases ledger control

Discounts Received

Date 20XX	Details	Amount £	Date 20XX	Details	Amount £
			01 Jun	Balance b/f	1,000
			22 Jun	Purchases ledger control	200
	Total			Total	

Select your account name from the following list:

Balance b/d, Balance c/d, Bank, Closing balance, Opening balance, Purchases ledger control

Task 1.6

Below is a list of balances to be transferred to the trial balance as at 30 June.

Place the figures in the debit or credit column, as appropriate, and total each column.

Account name	Amount £	Debit £	Credit £
Motor vehicles	26,300		
Stock	19,445		
Bank overdraft	11,463		
Petty cash control	300		
Sales ledger control	169,037		
Purchases ledger control	46,186		
VAT owing to HM Revenue & Customs	26,520		
Capital	17,019		
Loan from bank	16,500		
Sales	438,203		
Sales returns	4,660		
Purchases	264,387		
Purchases returns	674		
Discount received	1,200		
Discount allowed	1,840		
Wages	52,199		
Motor expenses	2,953		
Stationery	2,450		
Rent and rates	8,000		
Advertising	1,349		
Hotel expenses	1,224		
Telephone	1,599		
Subscriptions	360		
Miscellaneous expenses	1,662		
Totals			

Section 2

Task 2.1

Sales invoices have been prepared and partially entered in the sales day-book, as shown below.

(a)   Complete the entries in the sales day-book by inserting the appropriate figures for each invoice.

(b)   Total the last five columns of the sales day-book.

Sales day-book

Date 20XX	Details	Invoice number	Total £	VAT £	Net £	Sales type 1 £	Sales type 2 £
30 Jun	BGS Ltd	3105		2,625		15,000	
30 Jun	S Hopkins	3106	3,055				2,600
30 Jun	Kaur Ltd	3107	470		400	400	
	Totals						

Task 2.2

A supply of cardboard boxes has been delivered to Kitchen Kuts by Benson Boards. The purchase order sent from Kitchen Kuts, and the invoice from Benson Boards, are shown below.

Kitchen Kuts
14 High Street
Darton, DF11 4GX

Purchase Order No. KK1067

To: Benson Boards

Date: 7 July 20XX

Please supply 500 cardboard boxes product code 190467

Purchase price: £50 per 100, plus VAT

Discount: less 20% trade discount, as agreed.

Benson Boards

21 High Street, Darton, DF12 5PR

VAT Registration No. 398 3877 00

Invoice No. 3278
Kitchen Kuts
14 High Street
Darton, DF11 4GX

10 July 20XX

500	cardboard boxes product code 190467 @ £0.50 each	£250.00
	VAT @ 17.5%	£ 43.75
	Total	£293.75

Terms: 30 days net

Check the invoice against the purchase order and answer the following questions.

Has the correct purchase price of the cardboard boxes been charged? Yes or No?	
Has the correct discount been applied?Yes or No?	
What would be the VAT amount charged if the invoice was correct?	£
What would be the total amount charged if the invoice was correct?	£

Task 2.3

Kitchen Kuts codes all purchase invoices with a supplier code AND a general ledger code. A selection of the codes used is given below.

Supplier	Supplier Account Code
ABC Ltd	ABC32
Carlton Products	CAR14
Carter Couriers	CAR20
Farley Fans	FAR11
Johston Ltd	JOH18

Item	General Ledger Code
Kitchen doors	GL107
Kitchen equipment	GL110
Kitchen fans	GL113
Kitchen handles	GL117
Kitchen shelves	GL120

This is an invoice received from a supplier.

Carlton Products

36 Lower Dart Street,
Darton, DF13 4PX

VAT Registration No. 298 3997 00

Kitchen Kuts

14 High Street   20 July 20XX

Darton, DF11 4GX

80	Fancy handles for kitchen doors @ £0.70 each	£56.00
	VAT @ 17.5%	£ 9.80
	Total	£65.80

(a) Select which codes would be used to code this invoice.

Supplier account code	*Select your account name from the following list:* ABC32, CAR14, CAR20, FAR11, JOH18, GL107, GL110, GL113, GL117, GL120
General ledger code	*Select your account name from the following list:* ABC32, CAR14, CAR20, FAR11, JOH18, GL107, GL110, GL113, GL117, GL120

(b) Why is it necessary to use a general ledger code?

```
┌─────────────────────────────────────────────────────────────────┐
│                                                                   │
│                                                                   │
│                                                                   │
│                                                                   │
└─────────────────────────────────────────────────────────────────┘
```

Select the correct reason from the following list:

To help when bar coding an item of stock

To help when filing a financial document

To help trace relevant accounts quickly and easily

To help find the total amount owing to a supplier

Task 2.4

Shown below is a statement of account received from a credit supplier, and the supplier's account as shown in the purchases ledger of Kitchen Kuts.

B Grey Ltd
26 Winfield Road, Darton, DF15 8RL

To: Kitchen Kuts
14 High Street
Darton, DF11 4GX

STATEMENT OF ACCOUNT

Date 20XX	Invoice Number	Details	Invoice Amount £	Cheque Amount £	Balance £
1 April	308	Goods	6,000		6,000
3 May	342	Goods	1,600		7,600
7 May	355	Goods	900		8,500
26 May	368	Goods	1,100		9,600
1 June		Cheque		1,500	8,100

		B Grey Ltd			
Date 20XX	Details	Amount £	Date 20XX	Details	Amount £
1 June	Bank	1,500	1 April	Purchases	6,000
25 June	Bank	4,000	10 May	Purchases	1,600
			26 May	Purchases	900

(a) Which item is missing from the statement of account from B Grey Ltd?

Select your answer from the following list:

Invoice 308, Invoice 342, Invoice 355, Invoice 368, Cheque for £1,500, Cheque for £4,000

(b) Which item is missing from the supplier account in Kitchen Kuts' purchases ledger?

Select your answer from the following list:

Invoice 308, Invoice 342, Invoice 355, Invoice 368, Cheque for £1,500, Cheque for £4,000

(c) Assuming any differences between the statement of account from B Grey Ltd and the supplier account in Kitchen Kuts' purchases ledger are simply due to omission errors, what is the amount owing to B Grey Ltd?

£

Task 2.5

Kitchen Kuts sends BACS remittance advice notes to suppliers on the last day of the month following the month of invoice. Kitchen Kuts banks with Midway Bank plc and Robin Reed Ltd banks with Central Bank plc. Below is an uncompleted BACS remittance advice and an extract from Kitchen Kuts' purchases ledger.

Kitchen Kuts
14 High Street
Darton, DF11 4GX

BACS REMITTANCE ADVICE

To: Date:

The following payment will reach your bank account within 3 working days.

Invoice number	Credit note number	Amount £
	Total amount paid	

Robin Reed Ltd					
Date	Details	Amount	Date	Details	Amount
20XX		£	20XX		£
£16 May	Purchases returns credit note CN102	315	15 May	Purchases Invoice 125	1,650
29 May	Purchases returns credit note CN116	200	20 June	Purchases Invoice 189	2,918
30 June	Bank	1,135	29 June	Purchases Invoice 204	720
			10 July	Purchases Invoice 287	876

(a) To whom will the BACS remittance advice be addressed? (Select one)

Central Bank plc   Kitchen Kuts   Midway Bank plc   Robin Reed Ltd

(b) What will be the date shown on the BACS remittance advice? (Select one)

31 May   30 June   31 July   3 August

(c)   What will be the TWO items shown on the BACS remittance advice?

	✔
Purchase invoice number 125	
Purchase invoice number 189	
Purchase invoice number 204	
Purchase invoice number 287	
Purchase credit note number CN102	
Purchase credit note number CN116	

(d)   What will be the total amount paid?   £

(e)   Which of the following statements is true? (Select one)   ✔

	✔
The BACS remittance advice informs the customer of the amount payable to Kitchen Kuts	
The BACS remittance advice informs the supplier of the amount payable by Robin Reed Ltd	
The BACS remittance advice informs the customer of how much will be paid into its bank	
The BACS remittance advice informs the supplier of how much will be paid into its bank	

Task 2.6

On 1 July Kitchen Kuts delivered the following goods to a credit customer, Churchill Stores.

Kitchen Kuts
14 High Street
Darton, DF11 4GX

Delivery note No. 21765

Date: 7 July 20XX

Churchill Stores
20 The Mall
New Meldon
Surrey, SR11 5BS

Customer account code: CH152

---

100 cases of tinned fruit, product code F100.

The list price of the goods was £5 per case plus VAT. Churchill Stores are to be given a 20% trade discount and a 2% early settlement discount.

(a) Complete the invoice below.

Kitchen Kuts
14 High Street
Darton, DF11 4GX

VAT Registration No. 298 3827 04

Churchill Stores
20 The Mall
New Meldon
Surrey, SR11 5BS

Invoice No: 298

Customer account code:

Delivery note number:

Date: 1 July 20XX

Quantity of cases	Product code	Total list price £	Net amount £	VAT £	Gross £

Kitchen Kuts offers each customer a discount of 10% if any order amounts to £5,000 or over.

(b) What is the name of this type of discount?

Select your answer from the following list:

Bulk discount, Cash discount, Settlement discount, Trade discount

Task 2.7

The following is a summary of transactions with Etties Ltd, a new credit customer.

£3,525 re invoice 3070 of 12 July

£1,175 re invoice 3120 of 20 July

£752 re credit note 103 of 21 July

£846 re invoice 3134 of 27 July

Cheque for £1,800 received 29 July

Complete the statement of account below.

<table>
<tr><td colspan="5" align="center">Kitchen Kuts
14 High Street
Darton, DF11 4GX</td></tr>
<tr><td colspan="3">To: Etties Ltd</td><td colspan="2">Date: 31 July 20XX</td></tr>
<tr><td>Date 20XX</td><td>Details</td><td></td><td>Transaction amount £</td><td>Outstanding amount £</td></tr>
<tr><td>12 July</td><td>Invoice 3070</td><td></td><td></td><td></td></tr>
<tr><td>20 July</td><td>Invoice 3120</td><td></td><td></td><td></td></tr>
<tr><td>21 July</td><td>Credit note 103</td><td></td><td></td><td></td></tr>
<tr><td>27 July</td><td>Invoice 3134</td><td></td><td></td><td></td></tr>
<tr><td>29 July</td><td>Cheque</td><td></td><td></td><td></td></tr>
</table>

Task 2.8

The account shown below is in the sales ledger of Kitchen Kuts. A cheque for £1927 has now been received from this customer.

L Fortnum Ltd					
Date 20XX	Details	Amount £	Date 20XX	Details	Amount £
1 May	Balance b/f	3,525	2 June	Bank	3,525
20 May	Sales invoice 398	1,180	26 June	Sales returns credit note 110	1,128
30 June	Sales Invoice 401	3,055			

(a) Which item has not been included in the payment?

Select the correct item from the following list:

Balance b/f, Sales invoice 398, Sales invoice 401, Bank, Sales returns credit note 110

An invoice is being prepared to be sent to L Fortnum Ltd for £1080.00 plus VAT of £179.55. A settlement discount of 5% will be offered for payment within 10 days.

(b) What is the amount Kitchen Kuts should receive if payment is made within 10 days?

£

(c) What is the amount Kitchen Kuts should receive if payment is NOT made within 10 days?

£

Task 2.9

It is important to understand the difference between capital expenditure, revenue expenditure, capital income and revenue income.

Select and tick one option in each instance below to show whether the item will be capital expenditure, revenue expenditure, capital income or revenue income.

Item	Capital expenditure	Revenue expenditure	Capital income	Revenue income
Receipts from sales of goods to credit customers				
Receipts from cash sales				
Receipt from sale of Kitchen Kuts' delivery van				
Purchase of motor vehicle				
Purchase of goods for resale				
Purchase of stationery using petty cash				

Task 2.10

Financial accounting is based upon the accounting equation.

(a)   Show with a tick whether the following statements are true or false.

	True	False
Assets less liabilities are equal to capital		
Capital plus assets are equal to liabilities		
Capital less liabilities are equal to assets		

(b)   Classify with a tick each of the following items as an asset or a liability.

Item	Asset	Liability
Motor van		
Bank loan		
Money owing from debtors		

Practice assessment answers

Practice assessment 1 – answers

Section 1

Task 1.1

(a)   **Sales ledger**

Account name	Amount £	Debit ✓	Credit ✓
Durning Ltd	1,081	✓	
Perran & Co	4,089	✓	
Beacon Traders	5,922	✓	
Zelah plc	2,209	✓	

(b)   **General ledger**

Account name	Amount £	Debit ✓	Credit ✓
Sales	11,320		✓
Value Added Tax	1,981		✓
Sales ledger control	13,301	✓	

Task 1.2

(a)   **Purchases ledger**

Account name	Amount £	Debit ✓	Credit ✓
Mithian & Co	799	✓	
Bolster Stores	517	✓	

(b)   **General ledger**

Account name	Amount £	Debit ✓	Credit ✓
Purchases returns	1,120		✓
Value Added Tax	196		✓
Purchases ledger control	1,316	✓	

Task 1.3

(a)   **Sales ledger**

Account name	Amount £	Debit ✓	Credit ✓
Crossways Ltd	4,000		✓
Crossways Ltd	100		✓

(b)   **General ledger**

Account name	Amount £	Debit ✓	Credit ✓
Discounts allowed	100	✓	
Sales ledger control	4,000		✓
Sales ledger control	100		✓

(c)   **General ledger**

Account name	Amount £	Debit ✓	Credit ✓
Stationery	120	✓	
Value Added Tax	21	✓	
Rent	200	✓	

Task 1.4

General ledger

Account name	Amount £	Debit ✓	Credit ✓
Value Added Tax	7.42	✓	
Postage	12.00	✓	
Travel expenses	20.50	✓	
Office expenses	42.40	✓	
Bank	56.00		✓

Task 1.5

Discounts allowed

Date 20XX	Details	Amount £	Date 20XX	Details	Amount £
01 Jun	Balance b/f	640	30 Jun	Balance c/d	785
26 Jun	Sales ledger control	145			
	Total	785		Total	785
01 Jul	Balance b/d	785			

Rent received

Date 20XX	Details	Amount £	Date 20XX	Details	Amount £
30 Jun	Balance c/d	2,800	01 Jun	Balance b/f	2,350
			22 Jun	Bank	450
	Total	2,800		Total	2,800
			01 Jul	Balance b/d	2,800

Task 1.6

Account name	Amount £	Debit £	Credit £
Vehicles	15,390	15,390	
Bank overdraft	1,270		1,270
Petty cash control	112	112	
Inventory (stock)	9,345	9,345	
Capital	31,796		31,796
Drawings	6,290	6,290	
VAT owing to HM Revenue and Customs	2,317		2,317
Loan from bank	5,650		5,650
Purchases	22,685	22,685	
Sales ledger control	8,351	8,351	
Purchases returns	1,248		1,248
Sales	46,854		46,854
Purchases ledger control	6,382		6,382
Sales returns	1,685	1,685	
Discount received	817		817
Discount allowed	621	621	
Administration	18,341	18,341	
Advertising	4,057	4,057	
Hotel expenses	1,298	1,298	
Heating and lighting	1,836	1,836	
Rent and rates	3,494	3,494	
Travel costs	1,022	1,022	
Telephone	874	874	
Miscellaneous expenses	933	933	
Totals	–	96,334	96,334

Section 2

Task 2.1

Sales day book

Date 20XX	Details	Invoice number	Total £	VAT £	Net £	Sales type 1 £	Sales type 2 £
30 Jun	T Singh	4751	4,230	630	3,600		3,600
30 Jun	RMG Ltd	4752	1,645	245	1,400	1,400	
30 Jun	Wills Ltd	4753	329	49	280	280	
	Totals		6,204	924	5,280	1,680	3,600

Task 2.2

Has the correct purchase price of the batteries been charged on the invoice?	Yes
Has the correct discount been applied?	No
What would be the VAT amount charged if the invoice was correct?	£131.25
What would be the total amount charged if the invoice was correct?	£881.25

Task 2.3

(a) ELE10

(b) GL385

(c) EXP04, GL395

Task 2.4

(a) Cheque for £4,000

(b) Invoice 1752

(c) £800

Task 2.5

(a) Amici Ltd

(b) 30 April

(c) Purchase invoice number 1263

Purchase invoice number 1301

(d) £4,755

(e) The BACS remittance advice informs the supplier of the amount payable into its account at Western Bank

Task 2.6 (a)

	Sidbury Traders					
	29 Constitution Street					
	Mereford, MR11 4GT					
	VAT Registration No. 298 3827 04					

Bow Street DIY			Customer account code: BS152			
20 Penarth Road						
Bow Street			Delivery note number: 21765			
Ceredigion, SY56 2AW						
			Date: 9 July 20XX			
Invoice No: 1298						

Quantity	Code	Unit price £	Total £	Net amount £	VAT(17.5%) £	Gross £
10	PD124	56.00	560.00	448.00	74.48	522.48

(b)   £500.08

Task 2.7

	Sidbury Traders		
	29 Constitution Street		
	Mereford, MR11 4GT		

To: Broadsword Trading		Date: 31 August 20XX	
Date 20XX	Details	Transaction amount £	Outstanding amount £
10 August	Invoice 1301	450.00	450.00
12 August	Invoice 1370	1,210.00	1,660.00
21 August	Credit note 346	45.00	1,615.00
27 August	Invoice 1412	720.00	2,335.00
30 August	Cheque	405.00	1,930.00

Task 2.8

(a) Sales invoice 1262

(b) £5,190

(c) Bulk discount

Task 2.9

Item	Capital expenditure ✓	Revenue expenditure ✓	Capital income ✓	Revenue income ✓
Payments for purchases of goods from credit suppliers		✓		
Purchase of office equipment	✓			
Rent received				✓
Receipt from sale of vehicle			✓	
Receipts from sales				✓
Bank loan received			✓	

Task 2.10

(a)

Statement	True ✓	False ✓
Assets equals capital plus liabilities	✓	
Capital equals assets plus liabilities		✓
Assets minus liabilities equals capital	✓	

(b)

Item	Asset ✓	Liability ✓
Bank overdraft		✓
Office equipment	✓	
Money owing to payables (creditors)		✓

Practice assessment 2 – answers

Section 1

Task 1.1

(a)   What will be the entries in the subsidiary (sales) ledger?

Account name	Amount £	Debit ✓	Credit ✓
West and Webb	9,400	✓	
Kelly and Co	11,280	✓	
Bradley Delights	3,854	✓	
Burgess Wholesale	7,191	✓	

(b)   What will be the entries in the main ledger?

Account name	Amount £	Debit ✓	Credit ✓
Sales	27,000		✓
VAT	4,725		✓
Sales ledger control	31,725	✓	

Task 1.2

(a)   **Purchases ledger**

Account name	Amount £	Debit ✓	Credit ✓
Hanover Ltd	2,115	✓	
Lawson Ltd	470	✓	

(b)   **General ledger**

Account name	Amount £	Debit ✓	Credit ✓
Purchases ledger control account	2,585	✓	
Purchases returns	2,200		✓
VAT	385		✓

Task 1.3

(a)   Sales ledger

Account name	Amount £	Debit ✓	Credit ✓
RBL Ltd	6,000		✓
RBL Ltd	150		✓

(b)   General ledger

Account name	Amount £	Debit ✓	Credit ✓
Discounts allowed	150	✓	
Sales ledger control	6,000		✓
Sales ledger control	150		✓

(c)   General ledger

Account name	Amount £	Debit ✓	Credit ✓
Office expenses	80	✓	
VAT	14	✓	
Insurance	400	✓	

Task 1.4   General ledger

Account name	Amount £	Debit ✓	Credit ✓
VAT	11.20	✓	
Postage	20.00	✓	
Motor expenses	52.00	✓	
Office expenses	12.00	✓	
Bank	82		✓

Task 1.5   Telephone

Date 20XX	Details	Amount £	Date 20XX	Details	Amount £
01 Jun	Balance b/f	1,320	30 Jun	Balance c/d	1,599
26 Jun	Bank	279			
	Total	1,599		Total	1,599
1 Jul	Balance c/d	1,599			

Discounts Received

Date 20XX	Details	Amount £	Date 20XX	Details	Amount £
30 Jun	Balance c/d	1,200	01 Jun	Balance b/f	1,000
			22 Jun	Purchases ledger control	200
	Total	1,200		Total	1,200
			1 Jul	Balance b/d	1,200

Task 1.6

Account name	Amount £	Debit £	Credit £
Motor vehicles	26,300	26,300	
Stock	19,445	19,445	
Bank overdraft	11,463		11,463
Petty cash control	300	300	
Sales ledger control	169,037	169,037	
Purchases ledger control	46,186		46,186
VAT owing to HM Revenue & Customs	26,520		26,520
Capital	17,019		17,019
Loan from bank	16,500		16,500
Sales	438,203		438,203
Sales returns	4,660	4,660	
Purchases	264,387	264,387	
Purchases returns	674		674
Discount received	1,200		1,200
Discount allowed	1,840	1,840	
Wages	52,199	52,199	
Motor expenses	2,953	2,953	
Stationery	2,450	2,450	
Rent and rates	8,000	8,000	
Advertising	1,349	1,349	
Hotel expenses	1,224	1,224	
Telephone	1,599	1,599	
Subscriptions	360	360	
Miscellaneous expenses	1,662	1,662	
Totals		**557,765**	**557,765**

Section 2

Task 2.1

Sales day-book

Date 20XX	Details	Invoice number	Total £	VAT £	Net £	Sales type 1 £	Sales type 2 £
30 Jun	BGS Ltd	3105	17,625	2,625	15,000	15,000	
30 Jun	S Hopkins	3106	3,055	455	2,600		2,600
30 Jun	Kaur Ltd	3107	470	70	400	400	
	Totals		**21,150**	**3,150**	**18,000**	**15,400**	**2,600**

Task 2.2

Has the correct purchase price of the cardboard boxes been charged on the invoice?	YES
Has the correct discount been applied?	NO
What would be the VAT amount charged if the invoice was correct?	£35.00
What would be the total amount charged if the invoice was correct?	£235.00

Task 2.3

(a)

Supplier account code   CAR14

General ledger code   GL117

(b)

To help trace relevant accounts quickly and easily

Task 2.4

(a)

Cheque for £4,000

(b)

Invoice 368

(c)

£4,100.00

Task 2.5

   (a)   Robin Reed Ltd

   (b)   31 July

   (c)   Purchase invoice number 189

            Purchase invoice number 204

   (d)   £3,638

   (e)   The BACS remittance advice informs the supplier of how much will be paid into its bank

Task 2.6

   (a)

Invoice No: 298					
Quantity of cases	Product code	Total list price £	Net amount £	VAT £	Gross £
100	F100	500.00	400.00	68.60	468.60

   (b)   Bulk discount

Task 2.7

To: Etties Ltd			Date: 31 July 20XX
Date 20XX	Details	Transaction amount £	Outstanding amount £
12 July	Invoice 3070	3,525	3,525
20 July	Invoice 3120	1,175	4,700
21 July	Credit note 103	752	3,948
27 July	Invoice 3134	846	4,794
29 July	Cheque	1,800	2,994

Task 2.8

    (a)   Sales invoice 398

    (b)   £1205.55

    (c)   £1259.55

Task 2.9

Item	Capital expenditure	Revenue expenditure	Capital income	Revenue income
Receipts from sales of goods to credit customers				✓
Receipts from cash sales				✓
Receipt from sale of Kitchen Kuts' delivery van			✓	
Purchase of motor vehicle	✓			
Purchase of goods for resale		✓		
Purchase of stationery using petty cash		✓		

Task 2.10

    (a)

Assets less liabilities are equal to capital	True
Capital plus assets are equal to liabilities	False
Capital less liabilities are equal to assets	False

    (b)

Item	Asset or liability?
Motor van	Asset
Bank loan	Liability
Money owing from debtors	Asset